Reading Plus Comprehension

5

Therese Burgess

Illustrated by Celina Korcak

Reading Plus Comprehension 5

Text: Therese Burgess
Illustrations: Celina Korcak
Text design: Modern Art Production
Cover design: James Lowe
Production controller: Hanako Smith
Reprint: Siew Han Ong

Reading Plus Comprehension

Text © 2005 Cengage Learning Australia Pty Limited
Illustrations © 2005 Cengage Learning Australia Pty Limited

ISBN 978 0 17 012304 4

Cengage Learning Australia
Level 7, 80 Dorcas Street
South Melbourne, Victoria Australia 3205
Phone: 1300 790 853

Cengage Learning New Zealand
Unit 4B Rosedale Office Park
331 Rosedale Road, Albany, North Shore NZ 0632
Phone: 0800 449 725

For learning solutions, visit cengage.com.au

Printed in China by 1010 Printing International Limited
12 13 14 15 16 17 25 24 23 22 21 20

Contents

About this Book

Reading Plus Comprehension 5 is a comprehension workbook comprising thirty-seven units graded in difficulty. The steadily increasing complexity of language, concepts, exercises and questions reflects the growing skills of students throughout the school year. For this reason, students should progress through the workbook in a systematic rather than a random fashion.

The *Reading Plus Comprehension* series covers the full range of text types: narrative, description, recount, explanation, discussion, exposition, procedure, report and response. It also includes text forms such as poems, diagrams, maps, timetables and graphs, to encourage students' familiarity with other methods of conveying information.

Each unit of *Reading Plus Comprehension* has several types of comprehension questions and exercises, which concentrate on aspects of grammar, usage or vocabulary relating to the text. An extension activity at the end of the unit provides an opportunity for the student to use the text as a stimulus for reflection, research and composing.

The comprehension questions in this workbook are a mixture of literal, inferential and response.

- **Literal questions** ask students to find specific information in the text, to select correct information from a number of alternatives or to determine the truth of statements about the text.

- **Inferential questions** ask students to look into the text more deeply, to make connections that may not be obvious or to draw conclusions.

- **Response questions** ask students to make their own judgements about events or people in the text. They may also encourage students to draw on their own experience and knowledge to develop ideas about the text.

Tabs indicating question types enable ease of identification.

Reading Plus Comprehension includes a full set of answers, including suggested answers to response questions. These suggested answers are not the only correct answers, but both direct students towards areas they could cover and provide a model for the type of answer these questions require.

A checklist for key learning areas is included at the back of the book so that individual student progress may be monitored.

About this Book

For Teachers

Reading Plus Comprehension lends itself both to group and individual work in the classroom. It is not intended that students work on individual units without prior preparation. To gain maximum advantage from the workbook, the class should read and discuss the text before students begin individual work on the questions and exercises. The class can come together to discuss the answers to questions and to share responses.

The extension tasks can be approached in various ways. The students might do their research, planning and composing individually or in pairs, then come together to share their responses and to reflect on how well they have achieved their aims. Alternatively, the whole class might discuss the task and pool ideas before they begin individual work.

For Parents

Reading Plus Comprehension lends itself to home use for a student who needs extra help in developing comprehension skills. It can be used with a child who has difficulty in a particular area – answering inferential questions for example. Tabs are used to identify different types of questions so that a student can concentrate on their own area of weakness if they wish.

Children often make mistakes in comprehension because they do not understand what they are reading. Read the text with your child and encourage them to look up the meanings of unfamiliar words. Spend time discussing the text with them before they begin the exercises.

When using this workbook bear in mind that comprehension is not a test of a child's memory; it is a way of developing their understanding of written text. Always encourage your child to search the text for answers.

You can assist your child's learning by working together with this workbook.

Unit	Theme	Objective	Literacy	Maths	Social Studies	Personal Development	Science and Technology	Creative Arts
1	Melanie and Leo	Reads description and answers questions. Applies adjectives correctly. Supplies word meanings. Writes description of self	•			•		
2	The Fish King	Reads narrative and answers questions. Uses verbs correctly. Writes about wishes	•			•		
3	Brooke's Day	Studies timetable and locates answers. Compares to own day. Creates own timetable	•		•	•		•
4	Moths and Butterflies	Reads report and answers questions. Matches synonyms. Uses verbs correctly. Explores topic through research	•			•	•	
5	Nat's Story (I)	Reads literary recount and locates answers. Matches words and meanings. Writes a recount based on research	•		•	•		
6	Houdini	Reads historical recount and answers questions. Chooses exact meanings for words. Writes a response based on text	•			•		
7	Our Pets	Studies graph and locates answers. Chooses data to complete sentences	•		•	•		
8	Family Tree	Studies diagram of family tree and answers questions. Draws own family tree		•	•	•		•
9	Where Did Hot Chocolate Come from?	Reads explanation and answers questions. Finds words in text to match definitions. Sequences steps in making hot chocolate	•		•	•		
10	My Nanna	Reads poem and answers questions. Uses adjectives correctly to describe subject. Find synonyms for words in text. Writes own poem	•			•		•
11	April Fools' Day	Reads narrative and locates answers. Uses varying forms of the word 'fool' in sentences. Describes an April Fools' Day trick	•		•	•		
12	Jumari	Reads description. Puts sentences into correct order. Answers questions. Matches words to definitions. Writes letter	•		•	•		
13	Grandma's Schooldays	Reads description and answers questions. Compares with modern schools. Looks up word meanings in dictionary. Forms compound words. Researches school from past or another country and writes a report	•		•	•		
14	How to Make a Volcano	Reads procedure and locates answers. Finds synonyms for words from text. Writes a procedure				•	•	
15	Where Will We Go?	Reads discussion and completes table. Answers questions and makes own decision about issue. Finds exact meaning for words. Designs an advertisement	•		•	•		•
16	About Max – Skills	Finds ten mistakes in story and corrects them. Answers questions. Forms plurals. Selects correct meaning for common idioms				•		
17	Our Ears	Reads description and finds answers. Searches text for words matching definitions. Pairs 'ear' words with meanings. Writes a narrative about superpowers of hearing	•				•	
18	Strange Endings	Reads historical recounts and answers questions. Completes sentences with correct words. Finds dictionary definitions. Researches and writes report	•		•	•		
19	The Bullies	Reads narrative and answers questions. Completes cloze. Writes about a personal experience of bullying	•			•		
20	The Haunted House	Studies flow chart and locates answers. Chooses synonyms for words from text. Uses adjectives in sentences. With flow chart and word bank as stimuli, writes narrative	•					

Unit	Theme	Objective	Literacy	Maths	Social Studies	Personal Development	Science and Technology	Creative Arts
21	Ants	Reads report and answers questions. Uses dictionary to find 'ant' words. Researches a writes a recount of a day in an ant's life	•				•	
22	Nat's Story (2)	Reads literary recount and locates answers. Matches words and meanings. Researches and writes about life in Nat's day	•		•	•		
23	Christopher	Reads poem and answers questions. Determines the main theme. Forms adjectives from base word and suffix. Writes own poem.	•					•
24	Beavers	Reads report and selects answers. Chooses adverbs to complete sentences. Finds dictionary meanings for words. Uses homophones correctly. Writes about life as a beaver	•				•	
25	Scrambled Stories – Skills	Puts story into correct order and writes out. Matches text words with synonyms. Chooses names for pets. Sequences sentences to form story and answers questions about it. Pairs antonyms	•					
26	Tory's Good Idea	Reads narrative and selects correct words to complete sentences. Categorises jobs.	•			•		
27	Do High Buildings Sway in the Wind?	Reads explanation and locates answers. Studies picture of messy kitchen and lists jobs to be done. Searches text for words to match definitions. Finds odd-one-out in group. Researches and writes about tallest building in the world	•				•	
28	Leonardo da Vinci	Reads report and answers questions. Explains key phrases in own words. Matches antonyms. Designs own invention and writes about how it works	•		•	•		•
29	Happy Holidays!	Reads recount and locates answers. Forms compound words. Designs and writes a postcard	•		•	•		•
30	Teeth	Reads report and identifies correct answers. Categorises foods into good or bad for teeth. Unjumbles sentences. Makes a list of uses for teeth the Tooth Fairy collects	•			•	•	
31	Wizard Weekly	Studies front page of the newspaper and answers questions. Looks up words in alphabetical order. Arranges words in alphabetical order. Writes another article	•					
32	Working Children	Reads report and locates answers. Pairs adjectives with nouns. Finds dictionary meanings for words. Uses word bank as stimulus to write about working children	•		•	•		
33	Nat's Story (3)	Reads literary recount and identifies correct answers. Puts words in alphabetical order. Writes a narrative set in pioneer days	•			•		
34	Space Stories – Skills	Finds irrelevant information in paragraphs and answers questions. Matches beginnings and ends to make true statements. Finds out meanings of 'space' words and writes a report on one of them	•					
35	Food from the Bush	Reads report and completes sentences with correct data. Finds words in text to match definitions. Writes a narrative about an adventure in the bush	•		•		•	
36	How to Keep Tadpoles	Reads the procedure and answers questions. Puts water creatures into alphabetical order. Writes a procedure about taking care of a pet.	•			•		
37	More About Max – Skills	Finds mistakes in texts and corrects them. Answers questions about stories. Uses homophones correctly. Matches synonyms. Writes a description of best Christmas present. Makes a list of ideas for community service.	•					

Melanie and Leo

DESCRIPTION

Read the descriptions of the two children.

Melanie

Appearance: Brown hair. Blue eyes. Short. Slim.
Personality: Happy and bubbly. Likes jokes.
Easily bored. Active. Kind. Can be bossy.
Family: One brother, Scott and one sister, Emily.
Interests: Netball. Dancing. Playing piano. Running.
Collecting stickers.

Leo

Appearance: Black hair. Brown eyes. Average height.
Thin build.
Personality: Serious. Quiet. Good sense of humour.
Loyal to friends. Sometimes stubborn.
Family: Two brothers, Stuart and Patrick.
Interests: Chess. Basketball. Cricket. Playing guitar.
Running.

Literal

1   Write 'T' if the sentence is true, or 'F' if it is false.

     a   Leo is a very noisy boy.   _____

     b   Melanie's eyes are brown.   _____

     c   Leo has two brothers, Patrick and Scott.   _____

     d   Both children enjoy running.   _____

     e   Melanie is thin.   _____

     f   Leo plays the piano.   _____

     g   Leo plays cricket and basketball.   _____

     h   Leo's sister is Emily.   _____

     i   Melanie plays netball.   _____

Inferential

2 Express each answer in a complete sentence.

a Which words tell us that Melanie has a good sense of humour?

_____

b How do we know that both children are good to their friends?

_____

c What does 'easily bored' mean?

_____

Response

3 Decide to which child these adjectives apply. Some may not apply to either child. Use your dictionary.

cranky   talkative   jolly   cruel   trustworthy   funny   gentle
firm   shy   mean   teasing   generous   cheerful   angry

Melanie	Leo	Neither
_____	_____	_____
_____	_____	_____
_____	_____	_____
_____	_____	_____

Language Links

4 Match up the words in the box with the words from the text.

busy   quickly   thoughtful   caring   skinny   true   lively   strong-willed

a slim: _____   **e** bubbly: _____

b kind: _____   **f** easily: _____

c active: _____   **g** determined: _____

d serious: _____   **h** loyal: _____

Extension

Write a **description** of yourself. Include appearance, personality, your family and interests.

The Fish King

One day, Tom was fishing, when suddenly he felt a tremendous tug on his line. "Oh!" he exclaimed. "That must be a huge fish, I'll try to pull it in quickly." So Tom tried to wind in his line. But every time he managed to wind up a few metres of line, there was a short, sharp pull and the reel whizzed around. The fishing line whistled out into the water and the float bobbed up and down wildly. Tom wasn't making any progress!

Suddenly, there was a much stronger tug on the line and Tom was pulled off the wharf and into the water. Down, down, down, he sank through the blue-green water, the waving weeds and schools of darting silver fish. At last, his feet touched the seabed. There before him was a lovely, golden fish with scales of ruby red and emerald green. On its head was a crown of jade and pearls.

"Good morning," the fish said politely. "Tom, I am so pleased to see you! You are so kind to visit me. I shall grant you three wishes in return for your kindness."

Tom was delighted. Even though this visit to the Fish King had been an accident, he wasn't going to argue.

Literal

1 Choose the correct answer.

a Tom thought that he had caught a big fish because
- ○ he saw it on his line
- ○ he felt a really big tug on his line
- ○ he fell off the wharf

b Tom did not intend to argue because
- ○ he wanted to get his three wishes
- ○ he didn't understand fish language
- ○ he was afraid of the Fish King

c The Fish King's scales were
- ○ sapphire blue and ruby red
- ○ ruby red and emerald green
- ○ ruby green and emerald red

Inferential

2 Write the answers.

a Why do you think Tom realised he was talking to the Fish King?

_____

b What did the Fish King say was Tom's reason for coming?

_____

c Was Tom's being pulled off the wharf an accident? Give a reason.

_____

Response

3 Write the answers.

a What sort of palace might the Fish King have lived in?

_____

b Think of a good name for the Fish King.

_____

Language Links

4 Use each verb in the correct sentence.

| wondered | plunged | struggled | gasped | thanked |

a Tom _____ to pull in his fishing line.

b Tom _____ into the blue-green sea.

c He _____ when he saw the Fish King.

d The Fish King _____ Tom for his visit.

e Tom _____ what he could wish for.

Extension

If you were given three wishes, what would you wish for?

• _____

• _____

• _____

Brooke's Day

TIMETABLE

am

7:00	Wake up. Good morning! Get dressed and have breakfast
8:00	Music practice (drums)
8:30	Catch school bus
8:50	Arrive at school
11:00	Recess
11:20	School resumes

pm

12:30	Lunch
1:20	School resumes
3:00	Catch school bus
3:20	Arrive home. Have snack. Change clothes. Play
5:00	Do homework. Feed pets (two cats and one dog) Take dog for walk with big sister, Jo
6:00	Dinner
6:30	Winter – Netball practice. Summer – Swimming squad (if no sports practice, watch television)
8:00	Shower. Read in bed
8:30	Lights out. Good night!

Literal

1 Choose the correct answer.

a How many hours of sleep does Brooke have?
- ○ 8 ½ hours
- ○ 9 ½ hours
- ○ 10 ½ hours

b When does Brooke practise drums?
- ○ In the evening
- ○ In the morning
- ○ Both morning and evening

c How long does the bus take to reach school?
- ○ 10 minutes
- ○ 15 minutes
- ○ 20 minutes

d What chores does Brooke do?
- ○ Washing up and feeding the cat
- ○ Feeding the cats and fish
- ○ Feeding pets and walking the dog

Literal

2   Write 'T' if the statement is true, or 'F' if it is false.

- -

     a   Recess lasts for a quarter
         of an hour.   _____

     b   Brooke plays the piano.   _____

     c   Lunch lasts for fifty minutes.   _____

     d   Brooke's family has three pets.   _____

     e   Brooke has a bath at 8:00 pm.   _____

Inferential

3   Write either 'yes' or 'no'.

- -

     a   There is at least one other child in Brooke's family.   _____

     b   Brooke's home is a long way from school.   _____

     c   Brooke probably enjoys sport.   _____

     d   Brooke watches 1½ hours of television each night.   _____

     e   Brooke is very busy all day long.   _____

Response

4   Is your day like Brooke's or is it quite different? Explain.

- -

_____

_____

_____

_____

Extension

Write a **timetable** for the best day that you can imagine! It could be a day in the holidays or a birthday.

Moths and Butterflies

Moths and butterflies are common insects that live in your garden. They don't have skeletons inside their bodies as we have. Their 'skeletons' are on the outside – they don't have backbones, knee-bones or toe-bones, but instead have a soft body on the inside with a type of hard protective shell.

Butterflies can taste things through their feet. They often stomp up and down on a leaf, testing and tasting it to see if it is a good place to lay their eggs. Some butterflies lay their eggs all together, and others lay theirs in scattered bunches, which keeps the eggs safer from enemies that might enjoy snacking on them.

Butterflies and moths have a long hollow tube, just like a straw, that they use to suck up their food (flower nectar). The tube is called a proboscis and it can be curled away neatly when it is not being used. The longest proboscis belongs to Darwin's hawkmoth. It is about 35 cm long and the moth needs it to reach the nectar at the bottom of the deep flowers it feeds on.

Butterflies and moths have been fluttering about the skies for 140 million years. Unfortunately, modern times have seen many beautiful species become extinct. They have died out because forests have been cut down and their homes there have been lost.

Literal

1   Write 'T' if the sentence is true, or 'F' if it is false.

a   Butterflies and moths have hard outer shells.   _____

b   Butterflies have bones inside their shells.   _____

c   Moths have soft bodies within their shells.   _____

d   All butterflies lay their eggs in one big clump.   _____

e   Butterflies taste with their feet.   _____

f   The proboscis is like a sharp tooth.   _____

g   The longest proboscis is more than 30 cm long.   _____

h   A proboscis is used like a straw.   _____

i   Butterflies have existed for 140 000 years.   _____

j   The biggest moth is Darwin's hawkmoth.   _____

k   Butterflies and moths feed on nectar.   _____

Inferential

2   Write the answers.

   a   Why do butterflies sometimes stomp up and down on leaves?

   _____

   b   Why do some butterflies lay their eggs in scattered bunches?

   _____

   c   Why does Darwin's hawkmoth need such a long proboscis?

   _____

   d   Why is cutting down the forests so bad for butterflies and moths?

   _____

Language Links

3   Match up these words from the text with their synonyms.

| backbone | stomp | together | scattered | neatly | extinct |

a   tidily: _____   **d**   spread out: _____

b   spine: _____   **e**   stamp: _____

c   disappeared: _____   **f**   side-by-side: _____

4   Match the **verbs** in the word bank with the animals they best suit.

a   butterflies: _____   **e**   bears: _____

b   mice: _____   **f**   rhinos: _____

c   ducks: _____   **g**   eagles: _____

d   camels: _____   **h**   tigers: _____

scamper	plod
lumber	soar
flutter	waddle
charge	prowl

Extension

Use an encyclopedia or the Internet to find out the answers to these questions (your local garden centre may also be able to help):

• How can butterflies help your garden?

• How can you make your garden 'butterfly friendly'?

Report back to your class about your findings.

Nat's Story

HISTORICAL RECOUNT

"Hello! I'm Nat. The soldiers haven't arrived to take us to our quarters yet, so I can chat with you for a little time. I've just come ashore from that ship lying there at anchor in the harbour. Yes, that one. It's the *Kestrel*. Not very big, is it? You wouldn't think that three hundred souls could be packed in below decks, would you?

"How long was I at sea? Well, we left old England on August 5th, 1804 and what is it now? February? It's February the 3rd, is it? Yes, it's a long time to be cooped up with nothing to do but talk and fight sometimes. It's so good to feel the warmth of the sun on my back and to breathe the fresh air. Perhaps these sores on my legs will heal now.

"I'm really looking forward to a bath and to getting some clean clothes. Yes, I know I smell! You would too, if you hadn't changed your clothes or washed properly in six months!

"Were we well fed? Yes, we were… but a person gets mighty sick of salt beef and salt pork, meal after meal. And I don't care if I never eat rice or porridge again! Mind you, there were plenty of times when I couldn't eat because I was feeling so poorly. The ship was so heavily loaded that it rolled fearfully in storms. We were so afraid many times that we would sink.

"Why was I transported, you ask? I stole a chicken. Well, I'd best stop talking with you. The soldiers are coming. I wonder what life in this colony will be like?"

Literal

1   Choose the correct answer.

a   The *Kestrel* carried:
- ○   200 passengers
- ○   300 passengers
- ○   350 passengers

c   Nat is:
- ○   a sailor
- ○   a soldier
- ○   a convict

b   The voyage took:
- ○   six months
- ○   eight months
- ○   a year

d   The *Kestrel*:
- ○   has travelled from Australia
- ○   has travelled from England
- ○   is about to leave for Australia

2   Write 'T' if the sentence is true, or 'F' if it is false.

a   The *Kestrel* was a large ship.   _____

b   The *Kestrel* left England on 3 Febuary and arrived 5 August.   _____

c   The convicts did not have much to do.   _____

d   Nat had stolen a turkey.   _____

e   There were a number of storms during the voyage.   _____

f   Nat had a bath on board.   _____

g   The convicts were fed plain food.   _____

h   Nat was seasick at times.   _____

Inferential

3 What were some of the bad points of the voyage?

- _____
- _____
- _____

4 How can you tell that Nat is not just talking to himself?

_____

_____

Response

5 Think of a question you would like to ask Nat.

_____

Language Links

6 Match the words from the text with their meanings.

quarters   anchor   souls   cooped   poorly   porridge   fearfully

a   unwell: _____

b   living areas: _____

c   frightfully: _____

d   heavy weight which stops a ship from drifting: _____

e   people: _____

f   closed up: _____

g   boiled oats: _____

7 Use your dictionary to look up the meaning of 'kestrel'.

_____

_____

Extension

Write a **recount** of Nat's first day in the colony. Research Nat's time before you write. Share your recount with the class.

Houdini

Harry Houdini made his living in a very strange way. People would handcuff him, bind him with chains and padlocks, place him in a chest and throw him into a lake or river. Everyone would wait, hoping that he would appear again, but fearing that time might run out. The minutes would tick slowly by, and at last, when everyone was sure that he had been lost, he would appear, bursting out of the water, happy and smiling! A great cheer would erupt from the crowd. Houdini had won against the odds again!

Houdini was born in Hungary in 1874. His real name was Ehrich Weisz. When he was a young boy, he was very impressed by a magician's show. He began to practise tricks but as time went on, he developed a reputation as an escape artist. He didn't like being referred to as a magician.

Houdini visited Australia in 1910 and staged his famous underwater escape stunt in Melbourne. He was tied up and thrown into the Yarra River. As he sank into the murky depths, he managed to knock loose a body that had been caught in the mud for some time. Up, up, it rose to the surface. "Oh, no!" cried someone in the crowd, "It's Houdini!" But soon, the real and very much alive Harry Houdini appeared.

When Houdini visited Australia, his ambition was to be the first person to fly a plane here. He did manage to fly a plane, but unfortunately he was not the first – he was beaten by one day!

In 1926 Houdini invited people to punch him in the stomach to demonstrate how strong his abdominal muscles were. A volunteer obliged and punched him. Sadly, he suffered a burst appendix as a result and died.

Literal

1   Choose the correct answer.

- -

a   Which of these statements is true?

- ○   Houdini was a magician
- ○   Houdini was Hungarian by birth
- ○   Houdini was the first aeroplane pilot

b   Which of these statements is false?

- ○   Houdini was fifty-two when he died
- ○   Houdini changed his name
- ○   Houdini drowned in 1926

2   Write the answers.

- -

a   Into which Australian river was Houdini thrown? _____

b   What alarming event happened on Houdini's Australian visit? _____

_____

_____

c   Why was Houdini disappointed on his Australian visit? _____

_____

d   How did Houdini die?   _____

_____

Inferential

3   Why do you think Houdini didn't like being called a magician? Give a reason.

_____

_____

_____

Language Links

4   Circle the word in the brackets which best matches the word from the text.

a   appear   (float / show / amuse)

b   erupt   (flow / trickle / burst)

c   impressed   (excited / bored / shocked)

d   reputation   (act / name / part)

e   stunt   (job / joke / trick)

f   ambition   (desire / dare / ability)

g   demonstrate   (cheat / prove / ask)

h   obliged   (thanked / forced / agreed)

Extension

Imagine that you are in the crowd on the banks of the Yarra, watching Harry Houdini's escape attempt. Write a **description** of what you see and how you feel.

_____

_____

_____

Our Pets

GRAPH

These are the pets owned by the children of 4D.

rats	
axolotls	
guinea pigs	
mice	
rabbits	
birds	
fish	
dogs	
cats	

Literal

1 Write the answers.

a How many children own these pets?

    i rabbits: _____   iv cats: _____   vii birds: _____

    ii dogs: _____   v rats: _____   viii fish: _____

    iii axolotls: _____   vi mice: _____   ix guinea pigs: _____

b Which pet is most popular? _____

c Which pets are most uncommon? _____

d Rabbits are just as popular as _____ .

e There are as many pet mice as there are _____ .

f How many pets are there altogether? _____

Inferential

2 Fill in the blanks.

a _____ , _____ and _____ would be suitable

for children who live in apartments.

b _____ and _____ need hutches, while _____

and _____ live in tanks.

DIAGRAM

Johanna Foley – Patrick O'Shea

Brigid – James Goodwin   Mary – Harry Ross   Joseph – Emily Lucas

Olga   Doris   Cecil   Norma   Lily   Lloyd   John   James   Roy   Rose

Literal

1   Look carefully at the family tree and write the answers.

a   How many grandchildren did Johanna and Patrick have?   _____

b   Which of their daughters married Harry?   _____

c   How many daughters did Brigid and James have?   _____

d   How many sons did Joseph and Emily have?   _____

e   Who was Lloyd's father?   _____

f   How many cousins did James have?   _____

g   Who were Roy's brothers?   _____

h   How many nephews did Joseph have?   _____

i   Who did Emily Lucas marry?   _____

Inferential

2   Write 'T' if the statement is true, or 'F' if it is false.

a   Lily was Brigid's niece.   _____

b   Rose was Cecil's sister.   _____

c   John was Harry's uncle.   _____

d   Olga and Rose were sisters.   _____

e   Norma was Patrick's granddaughter.   _____

f   Doris was Rose's cousin.   _____

g   Lloyd's mother was Mary Ross.   _____

Extension

Using this family tree as a pattern, draw your own family tree for three generations.

Where Did Hot Chocolate Come from?

EXPLANATION

In 16th-century Spain, the newest craze was drinking hot chocolate. Cacao beans (from which chocolate is made) were brought by ship from Central America. The Indians of Central America had been making hot chocolate drinks for many years. They made their hot chocolate with water, not milk, and it was dark brown, spicy and bitter. At first, the Spanish people were not impressed with this strange drink. However, someone came up with the idea of adding sugar. As a result, drinking hot chocolate became popular in Spain, and quickly spread to England, France, Italy and beyond.

A cup of hot chocolate in those days was not at all like a modern one. It often had all sorts of odd flavourings, such as flower essences, wine and even eggs added to it. As well, the oily cocoa butter floated on the top. Sometimes, people stirred arrowroot or flour into the drink to absorb the oil. The result was probably a very stodgy drink.

Because cacao beans had to be shipped such a long distance, chocolate was an expensive drink and only the rich could afford it. The ordinary people generally drank beer, cheap wine or water. They probably wondered how this special chocolate drink tasted.

As drinking chocolate became popular, chocolate houses grew up in England. Rich men spent hours in them, drinking chocolate while they played cards for money, read the newspapers and shared the latest gossip. Rich ladies did not generally go to the chocolate houses, but enjoyed their hot chocolate at home, usually for breakfast.

Literal

1   Write 'T' if the statement is true, or 'F' if it is false.

a   Cacao beans were brought to Central America from Spain.   _____

b   Hot chocolate was first tasted in Europe in the 16th century.   _____

c   The first drinks tried by the Spanish were not sweet.   _____

d   Sometimes beer was added to the hot chocolate.   _____

e   Only the wealthy could afford hot chocolate.   _____

f   Chocolate houses became popular all over Europe.   _____

g   Flour was sometimes added to hot chocolate.   _____

2   Circle the best word in the brackets.

a   The Spanish added (butter / sugar) to their drinks.

b   Ordinary people often drank (coffee / beer).

c   Rich ladies enjoyed their coffee (in cafes / at home).

Inferential

3 Write the answers.

a How was a 16th-century cup of hot chocolate different to a modern one?

_____

_____

b Why was chocolate so expensive?

_____

_____

c Why do you think rich gentlemen enjoyed going to chocolate houses?

_____

_____

Response

4 Describe your favourite chocolate treat.

_____

Language Links

5 Search the text for words which have these meanings.

a	having a sharp, unpleasant taste	b	_____
b	liked by many people	p	_____
c	added to make the taste nicer	f	_____
d	soak up	a	_____
e	heavy and filling	s	_____
f	costs a lot	e	_____

Extension

Put these steps for making hot chocolate in order.

_____ Add one or two teaspoons of sugar.
_____ Pour the hot milk onto the cocoa.
_____ Add a little milk to the cocoa and sugar and mix to a paste.

_____ Finally, add whipped cream or marshmallows.
_____ Put three heaped teaspoons of cocoa into a cup.

Your class may like to make some hot chocolate. Don't forget the marshmallows!

My Nanna

POEM

My nanna rides a motorbike,
Dressed top to toe in leather.
She roars around the countryside,
No matter what the weather.

She made a parachute jump last year,
When she turned sixty-eight,
And now she wants to fly a plane!
I bet that she'll be great.

She swims, she skates, she surfs, she sails,
And her skiing is sublime.
She used to run the marathon,
But now she hasn't time.

Mum and Dad are disapproving.
They think she should take care,
And spend her time in knitting,
Or rocking in a chair.

But Nan is busy all day long,
With hardly a second free.
It's amazing how she always finds,
The time to be with me!

Literal

1   Write the answers.

a   How did Nan celebrate her birthday? _____

b   How old was Nan when she did this? _____

c   Which activity has Nan had to give up? _____

d   Why has she done this? _____

e   What new skill would she like to have? _____

f   What activity of Nan's is 'sublime'? _____

g   What water sports does Nan do? _____

h   What does Nan always find time to do? _____

Inferential

2 Match the beginning of each sentence with the correct ending.

a Nan wears leather when she rides her bike
- to look good.
- to keep cool.
- for protection.

b The person speaking in the poem is
- Nan.
- Nan's grandchild.
- Mum or Dad.

c Nan does all of these things because she
- has a lot of energy.
- is bored.
- likes to upset people.

d Mum and Dad
- are impressed by Nan's activities.
- are jealous of Nan's activities.
- are worried by Nan's activities.

Response

3 Circle the adjectives that you think describe Nan.

enthusiastic   boring   energetic   weak   busy   unhappy   cheerful

Language Links

4 Find synonyms from the word bank for the words from the text.

skilful   active   travels   unhappy   surprising   use

a roars: _____   **d** disapproving: _____

b sublime: _____   **e** busy: _____

c amazing: _____   **f** spend: _____

Extension

Write a short **poem** about one of your grandparents.

My _____

_____

_____

_____

April Fools' Day

NARRATIVE

"Tom!" called Jason, as he ran in through the school gate. "Why are you wearing odd shoes?"

"What?" replied Tom, glancing down quickly at his feet.

"April Fool!" shouted Jason, jumping up and down in delight.

"Oh, you really caught me out, Jason," said Tom. "I'd forgotten all about its being April Fools' Day. Have you caught anyone else out?"

"Yes, I played a cool trick on Susan this morning. I told her there was a big parcel for her downstairs. I said it was from her boyfriend. She leapt out of bed and rushed to see what it was."

"That was cunning." Tom's tone was approving. "Was she cranky with you?"

Jason pulled a face. "Yes, she was in a bad mood and she didn't speak to me again once she'd finished telling me how annoying I was."

"Never mind," Tom consoled him. "Let's see if we can catch someone else out. Look, there's Brooke. Watch this!"

Brooke was talking to Melissa and Holly as Tom strolled up to her. "Brooke, why are you wearing your pyjama top?"

Brooke smiled sweetly at Tom. "Oh, no!" she laughed. "You won't catch me out! My sister, Jo, has already done that. She told me that there was a unicorn in our garden and I went running to see before I remembered that unicorns are imaginary animals. Jo laughed and laughed at me. I'm not getting fooled again!"

Literal

1   Choose the correct alternative.

a   Jason's sister was:
   ○   Brooke
   ○   Susan
   ○   Jo

b   Brooke's sister was:
   ○   Holly
   ○   Melissa
   ○   Jo

c   Jason told Susan:
   ○   she was wearing odd shoes
   ○   there was a parcel for her
   ○   there were flowers for her

d   Tom told Brooke:
   ○   a unicorn was in the yard
   ○   the teacher wanted her
   ○   she was wearing pyjamas

2   Write 'T' if the sentence is true, or 'F' if it is false.

   a   Jason did not fool Tom.   _____
   b   Jason succeeded in tricking Susan.   _____
   c   Tom tried to trick Jason.   _____
   d   Brooke was fooled by Jo.   _____
   e   Jason did not try to trick Holly.   _____

Inferential

3 Write the answers.

- -

    a   What did Tom think of the trick Jason played on Susan?

_____

_____

    b   Did Susan like the trick Jason played on her?   _____

    c   How do you know this?

_____

_____

    d   Why didn't Tom's trick work?

_____

_____

Response

4 Which was the best trick? Why?

- -

_____

_____

Language Links

5 Use each of these forms of the word **fool** in the correct sentence.

- -

fooled   foolish   fooling   foolery   foolishly

a   They were _____ by the spy's wig and glasses.

b   The little girl looked _____ in her big sister's clothes.

c   "Stop all this _____ !" shouted the cranky man.

d   The boy grinned _____ when he was caught napping.

Extension

Have you ever had an April Fools' Day trick played on you or have you played one on someone else? Describe it.

Jumari

DESCRIPTION

Jumari is nine years old. She is slim and quite tall for her age. Her home is a small village on Lombok, one of the islands of Indonesia. Jumari's family has only two people in it now: Jumari and her mother. Her father died last year and her big brother, Supomo, who is fourteen, has gone to live with their uncle in a seaside village. Supomo has left school and his uncle is teaching him to be a fisherman. Jumari misses Supomo and wishes that he still lived at home.

Jumari's house is made of woven bamboo, and in places the walls and roof are broken and rotting, allowing the rain to come pouring in during the wet season. There isn't any gas, electricity or running water connected to the house. To get water for cooking and washing, Jumari and her mother must go to one of the wells in the village. Sometimes, Jumari makes four or five trips each day to get the water needed. Afterwards, her back and shoulders ache fiercely.

Jumari is in school at the moment and she hopes she will be able to stay there all year. In the past, there have been times when she has had to drop out for a while at rice planting or harvesting times to help her mother in the fields. But she was determined not to fall behind and asked her friends to let her copy their work and to explain things she did not understand. When she returned to school each time, Jumari found that she had kept up and was able to progress to the next grade.

Literal

1 Unscramble these sentences. Write either 'T' for true or 'F' for false.

a ten years Jumari is age of _____

b house live Jumari's three people in _____

c Lombok Jumari on lives island of the ___

d Supomo farmer is to learning be a _____

e school now Jumari is the in _____

f Jumari's is Supomo brother big _____

g sea lives Supomo beside the _____

h electricity Jumari's has house _____

2 Circle the correct word in each set of brackets.

a Jumari hopes to stay in school all this (month / year).

b Jumari has sometimes had to drop out to help her (brother / mother).

c Jumari was helped in her schoolwork by her (uncle / friends).

d Jumari (did / did not) fall behind in her work.

e The family fetched their water from the (river / well).

f The house is made of (bamboo / tin).

g The family grows (wheat / rice).

Inferential

3 Write each answer in a full sentence.

a What is Jumari's house like?

_____

_____

b Why do you think it is falling to pieces?

_____

_____

c Do you think Jumari has a hard life? Give a reason.

_____

_____

Response

4 Circle some adjectives which you think describe Jumari.

      lazy   determined   hard-working   rich   careless   poor

5 Find three ways in which Jumari's life is different to yours.

• _____

• _____

• _____

Language Links

6 Find the words in the passage which match these meanings.

a thin: _____   **d** joined to: _____

b coastal: _____   **e** hurt: _____

c falling apart: _____   **f** go on: _____

Extension

Write a **letter** to Jumari telling her about your life and asking some questions about hers. Share your questions with the class and then research the answers in groups.

Grandma's Schooldays

DESCRIPTION

In 1898, my grandmother, Olga Goodwin, started school. She was seven years old. Over the years she attended twenty different schools until she reached Year Three at the age of twelve. At this point, Olga refused to attend school any longer and left to become a milliner.

Gran usually walked to school with her brother, Cecil, and her sisters, Eileen and Doris. It was often many kilometres to school and they walked in all weathers, in blazing sun or pelting rain. When they attended a school at Ilford, there was a mountain between the school and their home in the railway workers' camp, so to get to school they had to climb over the mountain first!

Because the family was poor, the children did not wear boots for most of the year, but kept them for special occasions or for the coldest days of winter. Sometimes, the quickest way home was across a recently harvested wheat field, and the spiky stubble left behind cut their feet.

The lunches Gran ate at school were not like your lunches. There weren't any school canteens, and potato chips and juice-packs had not been invented. Children usually took whatever could be spared from home. This might be a cold baked potato, a chunk of home-made bread or a piece of cold mutton.

School did not always run for five days a week in those times. Gran attended a number of 'half-time' schools. These were set up in areas where there were not enough children to have full-time schools. A teacher shared his time between two small schools, with a half-day's ride between them. For one week, he spent two days in one and three in the other, and the next week, the reverse.

Literal

1 Write 'T' if the statement is true, or 'F' for false.

a   Children always rode horses to school.   _____

b   Children were required to wear shoes to school.   _____

c   Olga had one brother and two sisters.   _____

d   Children could leave school before the age of fifteen.   _____

e   Half-time schools were only open morning or afternoon.   _____

f   My grandmother's family was wealthy.   _____

g   Small schools closed on some days of the week.   _____

Inferential

2 Write a complete sentence to answer each question.

a What might Olga's father's job have been?

_____

_____

b Why were half-time schools set up?

_____

_____

c What would be the good points of half-time schools?

_____

_____

d What would be the bad points?

_____

_____

Response

3 Can you find three differences between the schools of Olga's day and modern schools?

• _____

• _____

• _____

Language Links

4 Look up the meanings of these words in the dictionary.

a milliner: _____

b stubble: _____

c mutton: _____

5 There are five compound words in the text. Find them and underline them.

Extension

Research a school from another time or another country and write a **report** on it. Compare your report with those of your classmates.

How to Make a Volcano

PROCEDURE

Materials

vinegar

small plastic bottle

bicarbonate of soda

sand and gravel

funnel

large tray

red food colouring

Instructions

1 Use the funnel to half fill the bottle with bicarbonate of soda.

2 Stand the bottle on a large tray.

3 Pack the gravel and then the sand firmly around the bottle. Pat it into a cone shape.

4 Pour a few drops of red colouring into a cup of vinegar.

5 Put the lava (vinegar mixture) into a small jug.

6 Quickly, but carefully, pour some of the mixture into the bottle.

7 Watch the volcano erupt as bubbles of carbon dioxide gas form in the bottle and force out the 'lava'.

Literal

1 Tick 'T' if the statement is true, or 'F' if it is false.

		T	F
a	Fill the plastic bottle with bicarbonate of soda.	○	○
b	The gravel and sand are used to make a mountain.	○	○
c	First sand and then gravel is packed around the bottle.	○	○
d	One cup of vinegar is needed.	○	○
e	Pour the vinegar over the sides of the volcano.	○	○
f	Pour the vinegar quickly from the bottle.	○	○
g	Bubbles of carbon monoxide form in the gas.	○	○
h	Use only a small amount of red colour.	○	○
i	You need a glass bottle.	○	○
j	The gas bubbles push out the 'lava'.	○	○

Inferential

2 Answer the questions.

    a Why is red colouring used? _____

    b Give a reason why this would be an activity to do outside.

    _____

    _____

3 Use 'before' or 'after' in these sentences to show the sequence of the procedure.

    a Pack the sand and gravel around the bottle _____ it is half filled with bicarbonate of soda.

    b _____ you pour the vinegar into the bottle, you need to add a few drops of food colouring.

    c Half fill the bottle with bicarbonate of soda _____ you do any of the other steps.

    d Arrange the gravel around the bottle _____ adding the sand.

Language Links

4 Match each word from the text with a synonym from the word bank.

> rapidly   place   drips   cram   thoughtfully   tightly   dye
> push   explode   container

a	fill: _____		**f**	drops: _____
b	stand: _____		**g**	carefully: _____
c	firmly: _____		**h**	quickly: _____
d	pat: _____		**i**	erupt: _____
e	colour: _____		**j**	jug: _____

Extension

Write a **procedure** for one of these:
- making an ice-cream sundae
- growing plants from seeds
- playing a favourite game

Where Will We Go?

DISCUSSION

"Alison! Braydon! Leah!" called Mum. "Come into the dining room. Dad wants to have a talk about where we should go for our next holiday." The children sat down around the big oak dining table.

"I know where we should go," began Braydon. "Disneyland! Cameron's family went last Easter and they had the best time."

Mum started to shake her head. "It would be very expensive for all of us to go. You know that we had to buy a new car this year... I don't think we could afford to go to Disneyland."

"Oh, I wish the stupid old car hadn't blown up!" muttered Braydon, looking glum.

"What about staying with Nan and Pop?" asked Leah. "I love riding old Nelly and helping to feed the chickens."

"Well," responded Dad, "they asked us to stay, but I think it might be too much work for Nan. Don't forget she had a knee operation six weeks ago. It might be better to postpone our visit. Alison, what suggestions do you have?"

"How about the beach? If we can't afford a beach house, we could get out the old tent and stay in a camping ground."

"That's an excellent idea," agreed Mum. "But the tent has been stored in the garage for a long time. I hope it doesn't have any holes in it!"

"Well, I guess we'll find out if it rains!" laughed Braydon.

Literal

1 Write the answers.

a Who was Braydon's friend? _____

b Why did the family need a new car? _____

_____

c What operation has Nan had? _____

d Why may the tent have holes in it? _____

_____

2 Complete the table showing the arguments **for** and **against** each suggestion.

	For	**Against**
a Disneyland		
b Nan and Pop's		
c the beach		

Inferential

3   Answer 'yes' or 'no'.

- -

    a   Nan and Pop probably live on a farm.   _____

    b   Braydon was disappointed not to be going to Disneyland.   _____

    c   Braydon doesn't stay upset for long.   _____

    d   Alison only wanted to stay in a beach house.   _____

    e   Mum was expecting rainy weather.   _____

Response

4   Where do you think the family should go? What suggestions would you make?

- -

_____

_____

_____

_____

_____

_____

Language Links

5   Match each word from the text with the best meaning from the brackets.

- -

    a   afford   (agree to / pay for / find time)

    b   glum   (angry / surprised / gloomy)

    c   postpone   (delay / cancel / forget)

    d   stored   (hung up / kept / hidden)

Extension

What is your favourite holiday destination? Write an **advertisement** for it. Remember to use words that will make people want to visit it. Draw a picture.

About Max

SKILLS – PROOFREADING

There are ten mistakes in this story about Max. Write your corrections in the box.

"Max!" called Mum, in an angry voise. "Have you bean touching Cindy's birthday cake?"

"No, I havent," said Max. "It must have been mouses."

"They would of been very big ones!" snapped Mum. "Why do you have choclate around your mouth?"

"I dont know," answered Max. "Perhaps I just bumped against the cake without noticeing."

"That's a likely storey," replied Mum. "Go to your room and stay their for half an hour."

CORRECTIONS

_____

_____

_____

_____

_____

_____

_____

_____

_____

Literal

1   Write the answers.

a   Whose birthday was it? _____

b   What excuse did Max give his mother?

_____

_____

c   How did his mother know that Max had eaten some icing?

_____

_____

Language Links

2   Complete the table.

Singular	Plural	Singular	Plural
mouse		deer	
foot		tooth	
cherry		fox	
goose		church	
baby		woman	
roof		volcano	

THE STORY CONTINUES...

While Mum was talking to Max, Cindy came into the room. Her eyes widened when she saw her birthday cake. The chocolate icing around the sides of the cake had been scraped away. There was even a little hollow on the top of the cake. It looked as though someone had scooped out some of the icing and then smoothed it over to hide what they had done. Cindy's eyes filled with tears and she rushed from the room. Mum stared at Max and he dropped his eyes to the floor. "Oh, dear," he thought.

Inferential

3   How did Cindy feel when she saw her cake?

- -

   O   delighted   O   upset   O   surprised

4   How might Mum have felt towards Cindy?

- -

   O   annoyed   O   disbelieving   O   sympathetic

5   How might Mum have felt towards Max?

- -

   O   angry   O   frightened   O   calm

6   Do you think Max is sorry for what he has done? Give a reason for your answer.

- -

_____

Language Links

7   We are told in the text that "Max dropped his eyes to the floor". This is an **idiom** and means that he looked down. Match these idioms with their meanings.

- -

| to make a face | to lose your head | to keep your chin up |
| to see eye to eye | to be all ears | to keep an eye on someone |

a   To be brave: _____

b   To panic: _____

c   To listen well: _____

d   To agree: _____

e   To watch: _____

f   To put on a strange expression: _____

Our Ears

DESCRIPTION

Our ears allow us to hear sounds of all types: the voices of our family and friends, the music we like, the sounds of nature, the noises of the city. As well, our ears help us to keep our balance and warn us of danger.

The part of our head that we call the ear is only the outer part of the organ of hearing. The ear has three parts. Sounds pass through the outer ear to the middle ear, which picks up the vibrations of the sound and transfers them to the inner ear. Here, they are changed into nerve signals that travel to the brain. The brain translates the nerve signals and tells us what sound we are hearing.

We measure sound in decibels. The sound of this page turning might be about thirty decibels, while the concert your big sister attended last night could have measured an ear-splitting one hundred decibels!

Our inner ear helps us to keep our balance. It has a number of semicircular canals that contain fluid, and this fluid moves when we move. Information about the fluid's movement is carried to the brain by nerves. The brain makes sense of this information and then sends messages to the muscles we need to keep our balance.

Have you noticed that a cat can move its ears and point them towards a sound? This is because a cat must be constantly on guard against danger and needs to know the direction from which a sound comes. Our ears don't move in the same way. Can you think why? It is because we don't have to protect ourselves in the same way. So, our ears sit close to our heads and don't move all around.

Literal

1   Tick 'T' if the statement is true, or 'F' if it is false.

		T	F
a	Our ears pick up sound vibrations.	○	○
b	The middle ear changes nerve signals into vibrations.	○	○
c	We measure sound in vibrations.	○	○
d	Loud music might measure one hundred decibels.	○	○
e	A cat moves its ears in order to hear better.	○	○
f	Our outer ear has fluid-filled canals.	○	○
g	Wiggling our ears makes us hear more efficiently.	○	○

2   Write the answers.

a   What does the middle ear do?

_____

b   Explain in your own words how our inner ear helps us to keep our balance.

_____

Inferential

3   Match the sounds with the decibel level.

> 30 decibels   40 decibels   60 decibels   120 decibels

a   A jet plane taking off: _____

b   The rustling of leaves: _____

c   Traffic in a busy street: _____

d   A door slamming: _____

Language Links

4   Look in the text for words which have these meanings.

a   harm: d_____

b   moves: t_____

c   quivers: v_____

d   cylinders: t_____

e   always: c_____

f   keep safe: p_____

5   Match up these 'ear' words with their meanings.

a	earmuffs	an ornament for the ear
b	earache	to talk without pausing
c	earrings	pain in the ear
d	earbash	an insect
e	earwig	warm ear coverings

Extension

Write a **narrative** about the day that you discovered you had superpowers of hearing. How did the discovery change your life?

Strange Endings

HISTORICAL RECOUNT

There are some strange but true stories in history of odd things that happened to famous people after their deaths. One of them is about William the Conqueror. This famous king died in the 11th century, and his body needed to be prepared for burial. An apothecary embalmed the body. ('Apothecary' is an old word for 'chemist'.) He did not do a very good job and after the body had been put into its lead coffin the gases from the decomposing body caused the coffin to buckle. In order to prevent the coffin from exploding, a hole was made to let out the gases. After they had been released the coffin was sealed up again. But despite this, something dreadful happened during William's funeral at Caen in France in 1087: during the service, the seal of the coffin gave way and the smell was so terrible that everyone rose and rushed from the church!

Another odd tale tells of the fate of Horatio Nelson's body. Nelson, the famous English admiral, was killed at the Battle of Trafalgar in 1805. Usually, sailors were buried at sea, but because Nelson was a famous admiral, it was decided to bring his body back to England. As it would take several weeks for the ship to reach England, some way had to be found to keep the body from decomposing. So it was placed in a large barrel, which was filled with either brandy or rum. Because of this, sailors have always called rum 'Nelson's blood'!

Another interesting story is that of Englishman Jeremy Bentham (1748–1832) who left instructions that after death, his body was to be dissected, stuffed and put on display. This was done, but his embalmed head did not look very attractive, so a wax one was put in its place. Dressed in some of his clothes, the body of Bentham was displayed in a glass case at University College, London. On special occasions the body was taken out and sat on a chair at meetings.

Literal

1   Write short answers.

a   Who embalmed William's body? _____

b   What is the modern name for this person's job? _____

c   Why was Nelson famous? _____

d   What was Bentham's job? _____

e   When was his body taken out of its display case? _____

2   Choose the correct answer.

a   Whose body was preserved in rum?
   ○   William's
   ○   Bentham's
   ○   Nelson's

b   Whose coffin opened?
   ○   Bentham's
   ○   William's
   ○   Nelson's

c   Whose head was replaced?
   ○   Nelson's
   ○   William's
   ○   Bentham's

d   Whose coffin was punctured?
   ○   Bentham's
   ○   the apothecary's
   ○   William's

Inferential

3   Choose the words from the word bank that complete the sentences.

bizarre   stomachs   fright   clever   solve

a   Resealing William's coffin did not _____ the problem.

b   The revolting smell turned people's _____ .

c   The sailors found a _____ way to preserve Nelson's body.

d   Bentham's instructions for his dead body were _____ .

e   People at meetings must have been given a _____ when they saw a body on one of the chairs!

Response

4   How would you have felt if you had been present at William the Conqueror's funeral?

_____

_____

Language Links

5   Look up the meanings of these words.

a   conquer: _____

b   embalmed: _____

c   decomposing: _____

d   barrel: _____

e   dissected: _____

Extension

Research and write a **report** on one of these:

- Egyptian mummies
- Otzi, the Iceman
- Sand mummies

The Bullies

NARRATIVE

Kevin was afraid to go to school. He knew that as soon as he walked through the school gate, someone would be waiting for him. They might grab his schoolbag and hide it, or open it up and scatter all the books in the dirt. Perhaps they might steal the best bits of his lunch and throw the rest in the garbage. Or they might threaten him until he handed over his lunch order money. Today, they might just trip him up and laugh as he fell. They could snatch the cap from his head and send it flying out through the school gate, to land on the road under the wheels of the cars and trucks.

Kevin had thought about telling someone. He'd started to say something to his brother, William, but Wills had become impatient with his stutter and had rushed off, saying, "Catch you later, Kev." He'd tried to think of a way to raise the subject with Dad, but the television was showing England versus Australia in the World Cup and Dad had shushed Kevin, and told him to wait till later.

Besides, Kevin remembered that the boys had warned him not to tell anyone. Telling would just mean that even worse things might happen to him. No, telling wasn't a good idea. Slowly, he walked into the kitchen, scuffing his feet against the tiles. "Mum," he whispered, "I feel sick."

Literal

1   Write each answer in a complete sentence.

- -

a   Why was Kevin afraid?

_____

_____

b   Name three unpleasant things that might happen to him.

_____

_____

_____

c   Why didn't William listen to him?

_____

_____

d   Why didn't his father listen to him?

_____

_____

e   What warning did the bullies give Kevin?

_____

_____

Inferential

2   Write 'T' if the statement is true, or 'F' if it is false.

   a   There is more than one bully.   _____

   b   William and Dad did not realise that something was wrong.   _____

   c   Dad thinks Kevin should sort out his own problems.   _____

   d   Kevin is too frightened to tell.   _____

   e   Kevin is really sick.   _____

3   Match up the beginnings and ends of these sentences.

   a   Kevin   can help to stop bullies.

   b   Bullies   must be stopped.

   c   Teachers   is very unhappy.

   d   Bullying   make children afraid.

Response

4   Imagine the next chapter of this story. Can you fill in the missing words?
        Choose words from the word bank.

Kevin's mother _____ that he was _____ about

something. Gently, she _____ him and he told her about his

_____ at school. She went with Kevin to see his _____ .

The boys and their _____ were asked to come to a

_____ at the school. Kevin did not have any more difficulty

with _____ .

| troubles |
| parents |
| worried |
| knew |
| headmaster |
| questioned |
| bullying |
| meeting |

Language Links

5   How do you imagine Kevin felt when his problem was solved?

   _____

Extension

Have you ever had an experience of being bullied? Perhaps another member of your
family or a friend has had this sort of trouble. Write a **recount**, telling what happened
and how it was solved. Share your recounts as a class. Can you decide together on
ways to prevent and deal with bullying?

The Haunted House

FLOW CHART

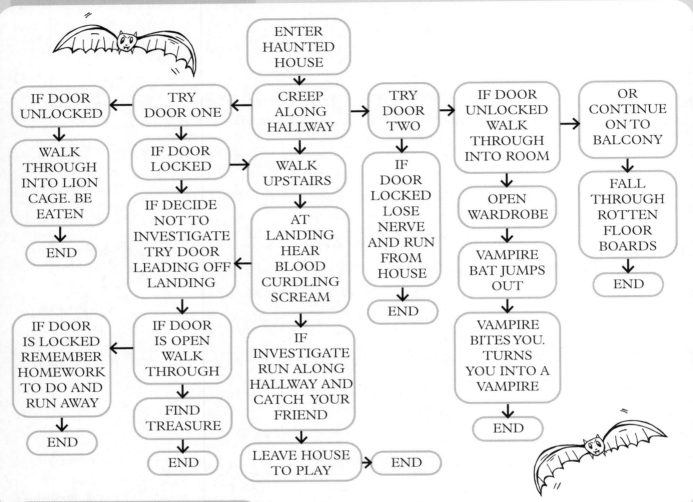

ENTER HAUNTED HOUSE → **CREEP ALONG HALLWAY**

CREEP ALONG HALLWAY → **TRY DOOR ONE**

TRY DOOR ONE → **IF DOOR UNLOCKED** → **WALK THROUGH INTO LION CAGE. BE EATEN** → **END**

TRY DOOR ONE → **IF DOOR LOCKED**

IF DOOR LOCKED → **IF DECIDE NOT TO INVESTIGATE TRY DOOR LEADING OFF LANDING** → **IF DOOR IS OPEN WALK THROUGH** → **FIND TREASURE** → **END**

IF DOOR IS OPEN WALK THROUGH → **IF DOOR IS LOCKED REMEMBER HOMEWORK TO DO AND RUN AWAY** → **END**

CREEP ALONG HALLWAY → **WALK UPSTAIRS** → **AT LANDING HEAR BLOOD CURDLING SCREAM** → **IF INVESTIGATE RUN ALONG HALLWAY AND CATCH YOUR FRIEND** → **LEAVE HOUSE TO PLAY** → **END**

CREEP ALONG HALLWAY → **TRY DOOR TWO**

TRY DOOR TWO → **IF DOOR LOCKED LOSE NERVE AND RUN FROM HOUSE** → **END**

TRY DOOR TWO → **IF DOOR UNLOCKED WALK THROUGH INTO ROOM** → **OPEN WARDROBE** → **VAMPIRE BAT JUMPS OUT** → **VAMPIRE BITES YOU. TURNS YOU INTO A VAMPIRE** → **END**

IF DOOR UNLOCKED WALK THROUGH INTO ROOM → **OR CONTINUE ON TO BALCONY** → **FALL THROUGH ROTTEN FLOOR BOARDS** → **END**

Literal

1 Write 'T' for true or 'F' for false in reponse to the following statements.

    a   The chart is meant to be read from right to left.   _____

    b   All the stories start with 'Creep along hallway'.   _____

    c   There are three doors you can try.   _____

    d   The lion is hiding in the wardrobe.   _____

    e   Your friend is chased by a vampire.   _____

    f   When you are on the landing you hear someone scream.   _____

    g   The stair boards are rotten.   _____

    h   There are some real dangers in the house.   _____

2 Write about what may happen to you in each of these situations.

    a   You decide to investigate the scream. _____

_____

b   You open the wardrobe. _____

_____

c   You walk out onto the balcony. _____

_____

d   Door Two is locked. _____

_____

e   You try the door off the landing. _____

_____

f   Door One is unlocked. _____

_____

Language Links

3   Circle the word from the bracket which is a synonym for the word from the text.

a   unlocked: (fastened / unfastened / untouched)

b   nerve: (worry / rudeness / courage)

c   rotten: (crumbling / dirty / gloomy)

d   decide: (tell / refuse / choose)

e   investigate: (flee / search / trespass)

f   balcony: (roof / pantry / verandah)

4   Put each of these adjectives into the best sentence.

blood-curdling   spine-chilling   heart-stopping   faint-hearted

a   They were frozen by a _____ scream from upstairs.

b   Fearfully they listened to the _____ noise of chains rattling.

c   The _____ boys charged from the old house.

d   A peal of _____ laughter broke the silence.

Extension

Write a **narrative** from the chart. Here are some good words and phrases to get you started.

terrified   hearts thumping   chilly moonlight   shrieking   cackling
creaking stairs   gloomy   cobwebs   dark clouds   lightning   screams

Ants

REPORT

Ants are social insects that live in colonies. Each ant has its own particular job in the colony and everyone works cooperatively. The queen ant, which is much bigger than the other ants, lays all the eggs. She has special handmaiden ants that feed and groom her and keep her comfortable. They take the eggs to the nurseries where nursemaid ants care for them. They also guard the eggs against predators that might eat them. These predators can be birds, animals or other ants.

Some ants are worker ants. Their job is to search for food and repair damage to the nest caused by dogs, cats or even you, digging in the garden! Other ants are soldier ants. Their job is to protect the colony from invasion. These soldier ants are very brave and will even attempt to prevent humans from harming the nest by nipping them with their pincers!

The next time you see an ant, look at it closely. Ants are incredibly strong. If you were an ant, you would be able to lift about fifty times your own weight. You could even lift up the family car while Dad changed a tyre!

Literal

1   Tick 'T' if the statement is true, or 'F' if it is false.

		T	F
a	Ants live together in groups.	○	○
b	An ant colony will have several queens.	○	○
c	Soldier ants guard the eggs in the nurseries.	○	○
d	Each ant has a particular task.	○	○
e	Ants will flee from their nests if danger threatens.	○	○
f	Only the queen ant lays eggs.	○	○
g	The handmaiden ants search for food.	○	○
h	If a nest is harmed, the worker ants will repair it.	○	○
i	The baby ants are cared for by the handmaiden ants.	○	○
j	The worker ants clean the queen.	○	○

Inferential

2 Imagine you were as strong as an ant. If you weighed 30 kg, how heavy a weight could you lift?

    ○   80 kg   ○   150 kg   ○   1500 kg   ○   15000 kg

3 Using the clues in the paragraph, what do you think a 'predator' is?

Response

4 Which ants have the most important job? Give a reason for your answer.

5 If you were an ant, how could you describe yourself? Tick as many boxes as you wish.

    ○ frightened   ○ busy   ○ strong   ○ lazy   ○ brave   ○ useless

Language Links

6 Match each word from the text with its synonym.

a	pincers	fearless
b	invasion	jaws
c	colonies	attack
d	brave	harm
e	damage	settlements

7 What are these 'ant' words? (Your dictionary will help.)

a   ant _ _ _ _ _   a swift, deer-like animal   d   ant _ _ _   the horn of a deer

b   ant _ _ _ _ _   an animal which feeds on ants   e   ant _ _ _ _   a song

f   ant _ _ _ _   a word which is the opposite of another

c   Ant _ _ _ _ _ _   around the South Pole

Extension

Write a **recount** titled "A Day in the Life of an Ant."
Research ants before you write and decide which type of ant you are.
Share your recount with the class.

Nat's Story (2)

HISTORICAL RECOUNT

"Hello! Remember me? It's Nat. It must be six months since I talked to you.

"How have things gone with me? They've gone very well and no mistake! You can see that I'm a big, strong boy, can't you? I was sure they would put me to work cutting stone blocks for the new buildings. Or even worse, I feared they might assign me to a road-gang. That's backbreaking work, out in all weather, and the overseers are real devils! But, do you know, the day after the *Kestrel* docked, Mr Price came looking for a servant. He has a general store in Beech Street and he needed a smart young fellow to help him. 'That's me,' I told him, and so he took me on.

"Well, my eyes widened when I walked in the door, I can tell you! The shop sells everything from padlocks to penknives, from shawls to spices, from muskets to mustard, from meat choppers to corsets. And was it crowded! I'm busy from dawn to dusk, fetching and carrying. I do the weighing and bagging of food. When I'm working I listen to the conversation. A smart fellow can learn a lot if he keeps his ears open. I listen and I make my plans.

"What are my plans? Well, I'll be through my term in five years and I'm going to head west then. Over the Blue Mountains I'll go, to the good land and I'll get me a little farm. Yes, sir! That's what I'll do."

"Well, it's been great to chat to you, sir, but I'd best go. I'm off to the markets to do the shopping for the cook. It makes a nice break from the shop. Goodbye, sir!"

Literal

1   Tick 'T' if the statement is true, or 'F' if it is false.

		T	F
a	Nat spent some time cutting stone blocks.	○	○
b	Nat is Mr Price's employee.	○	○
c	Nat's term will finish in four years.	○	○
d	Mr Price's store is in Beach Street.	○	○
e	Nat hopes to farm some land one day.	○	○
f	The shop has long hours of business.	○	○
g	The shop sells many different goods.	○	○

2   Write the answers.

a   List some of the goods sold in Mr Price's shop. _____

_____

b   Where does Nat hope to get a farm? _____

_____

c When will he do this? _____

_____

Inferential

3 Choose the correct answer.

a Why does Nat like listening to the conversations in the shop?
- ○ It gives him a break from his work
- ○ He learns a lot about the outside world
- ○ He's just a curious boy

b Which words tell us the shop does good business?
- ○ 'my eyes widened'
- ○ 'it sells everything'
- ○ 'was it crowded'

4 How was Mr Price's shop different to the shops of today?

_____

Response

5 How would you like to have Nat's job? Explain your reasons.

_____

Language Links

6 Match these words from the text with their meanings.

penknife   assign   musket   corset   shawl   mustard

a to give someone a job: _____

b an undergarment that gives support: _____

c a small knife: _____

d an old-fashioned gun: _____

e a yellow paste put on meat: _____

f a covering for the shoulders: _____

Extension

Imagine you are Nat. Write a **recount** of your day. Remember that the time is around 1800. There won't be any cars or computers! You may like to do some research first to discover what people wore and ate.

Christopher

POEM

I'm Christopher the cane toad,
My face is not too pretty,
Most people do not like me,
That really is a pity.

My personality's sparkling,
My manners are refined,
This unattractive exterior,
Hides a brilliant mind.

I'm brave and strong and tricky,
I never shirk a dare,
I'm absolutely charming,
I'm loyal, kind and fair.

I'm talented at music,
My sporting skills are swell,
I sing and dance superbly,
I'm modest, too, as well.

Next time you see a cane toad,
Just bear these words in mind,
Look beneath the warty surface,
And who knows what you'll find!

Literal

1   Write 'T' or 'F' in response to the following statements.

   a   Christopher says he is not very smart.   _____

   b   Christopher says that he has lovely manners.   _____

   c   Christopher thinks he is handsome.   _____

   d   Christopher claims he sings sweetly.   _____

   e   Christopher says he is bossy.   _____

   f   Christopher knows most people don't like him.   _____

   g   Christopher says he doesn't like dancing.   _____

   h   Christopher is not good at sports.   _____

2   Find the words in the poem which tell us these things about Christopher.

   a   He is happy and lively: _____

   b   He is polite: _____

   c   He is smart: _____

   d   He will try anything: _____

   e   He would be a good friend: _____

   f   He is a good sportsman: _____

   g   He is not proud: _____

Inferential

3   What is the main idea of the poem? Which proverb sums this idea up?

- ○   Look before you leap.
- ○   Never judge a book by its cover.
- ○   Never kiss a frog.

Response

4   Which three of Christopher's qualities impress you the most?
     Give a reason for each choice.

_____

_____

_____

Language Links

5   Add one of the endings to the beginnings below to form adjectives. (Some, but not all, are
     from the text.)

> ful   y   ing   ous   ive   al   eous   ant

a   attract_____   e   adventur_____

b   wart_____   f   charm_____

c   harm_____   g   courag_____

d   import_____   h   music_____

Extension

Try writing your own **poem**. Use one of these beginnings or make up your own.

- •   I'm Engelbert the elephant…
- •   I'm Gertrude the gorilla…
- •   I'm Theodore the tiger…

Beavers

REPORT

Beavers are amphibious rodents that live in Europe, Asia and North America. You probably know that beavers build dams, but have you ever wondered why? Beavers like to have a nice deep swimming pool, with lots of 'pantry' space for storing branches, their winter food. So if the river is not deep enough, beavers build a dam to trap more water. With their extremely sharp incisor (front) teeth, they chew through logs and branches. Then they drag them into position, raising the level of the barrier until the stream slows down.

Beavers are funny, clumsy animals on land, but in the water, they swim strongly and skilfully. They use their front paws like canoe paddles and their broad, flat tails are just like boat rudders. Their thick coat of fur is well oiled and keeps the water out.

Beavers live together in families. Upstream of their dams, they build cosy lodges, tunnelled into the bank and lined with aspen and willow branches. The lodges have many rooms, connected by tunnels. The entrance to the lodge is deep down under the water to keep it safe from enemies.

When beavers sense danger they smack the water with their tails to alert other members of their family. A mother beaver will grasp a baby in her teeth and swim away quickly. Beavers are interesting animals. Look for them next time you visit the zoo.

Literal

1 Choose the best answer.

a   Beavers build dams:
- ○ for protection against enemies
- ○ to make a home
- ○ to make the water deeper

b   Beavers are:
- ○ clumsy on land and water
- ○ graceful on land, clumsy in water
- ○ clumsy on land, graceful in water

c   The beaver's coat is oiled:
- ○ to keep it free of dirt
- ○ to keep the water out
- ○ to keep it free of tangles

d   The beaver's lodge is:
- ○ underwater
- ○ underground
- ○ on land

2 Write each answer.

a   What is the name of the sharp front teeth? _____

b   Why is the entrance to the lodge underwater?

_____

_____

c   Name two things which beavers do in a dangerous situation.

_____

_____

Inferential

3   Select the correct adverb to complete each sentence.

   a   The beaver's coat grows _____ .

   b   Beavers build dams very _____ .

   c   Mother beavers escape _____ .

   d   Beavers can swim very _____ .

strongly

speedily

skilfully

thickly

Language Links

4   Look up these words in the dictionary and write down their meanings.

   a   pantry: _____

   b   lodge: _____

   c   rodent: _____

   d   rudder: _____

5   Use these homophones in the correct sentence.

paws   pause   fur   fir   tails   tales

   a   The beaver's _____ keeps it warm in winter.

   b   The _____ of beavers help them to swim strongly.

   c   The beaver uses its _____ to place logs on the dam.

   d   The beaver did not _____ while building the dam.

   e   There were many _____ trees on the bank of the river.

   f   Have you read many _____ about beavers?

Extension

Imagine you are a beaver and write a **recount** about a day in your life.

Scrambled Stories

SKILLS – SEQUENCING

This story is not written in the correct sequence. Write it out again, putting all the sentences into the correct order. The first sentence is underlined to help you start.

Tosca rushed at Cassie. She thinks she is a fierce lion and if a dog comes into our garden, she rushes at it, hissing and snarling. <u>We have a naughty kitten named Tosca.</u> One day, Cassie, a black Labrador, wandered into our garden. She didn't come down until dinnertime. Tosca was so amazed that she raced up the nearest tree. Cassie was not frightened of a small, grey kitten and going up to Tosca, gave her a huge lick. She doesn't realise that she is a weak little kitten and that she should hide.

_____

_____

_____

_____

Language Links

1   Match these words from the text with their synonyms.

| rushed | fierce | snarling | wandered | amazed | frightened |

a   growling: _____

b   surprised: _____

c   strayed: _____

d   wild: _____

e   afraid: _____

f   charged: _____

2   Think up some good names for these pets. Remember that proper names need capital letters.

a   a rabbit: _____

b   a dog: _____

c   a bird: _____

d   a fish: _____

Language Links

3   Can you put this story into its correct sequence? Number each sentence.

_____ Half-way down, she narrowly missed a parked car.

_____ She did not know very much about skating.

_____ Anna was given skates for her birthday.

_____ Foolishly, Anna went to the top of a high and very steep hill.

_____ Anna needed stitches in her head.

_____ She banged her head very badly.

_____ Near the bottom, she ran into the gutter.

_____ But then, she began to go faster and faster down the hill.

_____ They took her to the hospital.

_____ She started off slowly.

_____ Anna's parents were called.

Inferential

4   Write the answers.

a   How was Anna's behaviour foolish?

_____

b   What lesson can you learn from what Anna did?

_____

_____

c   If you were teaching your younger brother or sister to skate, what advice would you give them?

_____

_____

d   How do you think Anna's parents felt when they were called?

_____

Language Links

5   Match each word from the text with its antonyms.

high	top	began	slowly	foolishly	bottom

a   rapidly: _____   **d**   wisely: _____

b   base: _____   **e**   summit: _____

c   finished: _____   **f**   low: _____

Tory's Good Idea

NARRATIVE

"I wish I could be the mother and stay home all day!" grumbled Tory, as she left for school one wet, grey morning.

"Well," said Mum, "we'll do a swap one day in the holidays, if you like. You can be Mum and I'll be Tory."

"Oh, cool!" replied Tory. "I get to watch TV all day and eat anything I like."

Mum smiled, but didn't say anything further.

One day in the long holidays, Tory's mother woke her up. "This is our day for swapping," she reminded Tory. "Remember, I'm going to be you, so I think I'll play with my friends. I'm going to Jenny's house to swim and have lunch. Dad is here to keep you company. Here's a list of everything you have to do. Bye!" And with that, she hurried out the door, chuckling to herself. Tory looked at the list.

"Oh dear," she said to herself. "I don't think this was such a good idea!"

Literal

1   Answer each question in a full sentence.

a   What two things did Tory think her mother did at home?

_____

b   When did Tory and her mother swap places?

_____

c   How was Mum planning to spend her day?

_____

Inferential

2   Choose the correct word in each set of brackets.

a   It was clear that (Mum / Tory) got the best deal.

b   Mum chuckled because Tory (had a good idea / had no idea) of what Mum's day was really like.

c   At the end of the day Tory would probably feel (exhausted / delighted).

3 This is the list of Tory's jobs for the day. Sort them out into kitchen jobs, bathroom jobs and so on.

Dust loungeroom furniture
Vacuum carpet in loungeroom
Clean bath and bathroom basin
Empty waste-paper bins

Make beds
Wash kitchen floor
Do ironing
Wash bathroom floor

Feed pets
Wash up
Change towels

Do washing
Vacuum bedrooms
Do shopping
Make Dad's lunch

KITCHEN	BATHROOM	BEDROOM	LOUNGE ROOM	LAUNDRY	OTHER

4 How many of these jobs can you do? List them.

_____

_____

Extension

Here is a very messy kitchen. Make a list of all the things you would need to do to clean it up.

Do High Buildings Sway in the Wind?

EXPLANATION

Have you ever watched large trees swaying violently in high winds? Powerful gusts of wind can break off branches and even uproot trees.

Have you ever wondered about what happens to very high buildings in strong winds? Do they sway in the same way? Could an extremely fierce wind damage a tall building?

Most skyscrapers can actually sway a few metres in either direction without suffering any damage. However, if a building moves too much, the occupants will feel this and may be very uncomfortable. They could suffer from motion sickness! So builders attempt to construct buildings in such a way that they cannot move very much at all.

One way of keeping skyscrapers from moving is to strengthen the mid-section of the building. In older buildings this was done by making the area around the central lift shafts very strong. These days, engineers plan to have concrete cores in the centre of buildings.

A modern technique for preventing skyscrapers from moving is to have a very large weight on a top floor of the building. This weight, which may weigh 400 tonnes, is connected to a computer system. The system senses which way the wind will push the building and moves the weight in the opposite direction. In this way, the building is kept motionless.

Literal

1   Tick 'T' if the statement is true, or 'F' if it is false.

		T	F
a	Strong winds can rip up trees.	○	○
b	Powerful winds can topple buildings.	○	○
c	A small sideways movement will not harm a tall building.	○	○
d	Movement of a building can make people sick.	○	○
e	Builders once constructed very strong lifts.	○	○
f	Builders now make strong central cores in buildings.	○	○
g	The top floor weight may be up to 400 kg.	○	○
h	The weight moves with the wind.	○	○
i	A computer measures the wind and moves the weight.	○	○

Inferential

2 Write the answers.

a Why do builders try to keep high buildings from moving too much?

_____

_____

b Explain in your own words how a weight at the top of the building helps to keep the building from moving too much.

_____

_____

Response

3 How would you like to live in a multi-storey building? Explain why you feel this way.

_____

_____

Language Links

4 Search the text for words which have these meanings.

a with great force: _ _ _ _ _ _ _ _ _ _

b strong bursts: _ _ _ _ _ _

c harm or spoil: _ _ _ _ _ _ _

d people staying in a particular place: _ _ _ _ _ _ _ _ _

e parts in the middle: _ _ _ _ _

f way of doing something: _ _ _ _ _ _ _ _ _ _

g joined to: _ _ _ _ _ _ _ _ _

5 Circle the **odd one out** in each line.

a skyscraper, mansion, escalator, cabin   **c** pantry, cellar, laundry, gable

b engineer, sculptor, architect, builder   **d** farm, city, town, village

Extension

Use an encyclopedia or the Internet to find out where the tallest building in the world is and how many storeys it has. Write a brief **description** of it.

Leonardo da Vinci

REPORT

In the 15th century, there lived a young man who had a very lively and curious mind. He filled dozens of notebooks with designs for marvellous inventions, including helicopters, snorkels, parachutes, machine guns, submarines and flying machines. It was to be another four hundred years before these inventions were thought up or built by someone else. The name of this young man with an amazing imagination was Leonardo da Vinci.

Leonardo is best remembered for two of his paintings. They are "The Last Supper" and the "Mona Lisa". Both of these paintings were unusual in their day because the people in them look very natural and real. Leonardo spent much of his time wandering about the cities of Rome, Florence and Milan, watching people and drawing them in his notebooks. As a result, his paintings look very lifelike.

Leonardo liked everything he did to be perfect. He often failed to finish paintings because he decided they weren't good enough and started another project instead. In fact, on his deathbed his last words were that he had failed God and man by not striving harder after perfection! Leonardo hasn't left many paintings for us to enjoy and appreciate. What a pity this is!

Leonardo da Vinci

Literal

1   Which one of these statements about Leonardo is true?

- O   Leonardo designed the first microwave.
- O   Many of Leonardo's paintings were not good.
- O   Leonardo painted "The Last Summer".
- O   Leonardo's paintings were very lifelike.

2   Which one of these statements about Leonardo is false?

- O   Leonardo invented a flying machine.
- O   Leonardo lived in Italy in the 15th century.
- O   Leonardo's wife was called Mona Lisa.
- O   Leonardo did not leave many paintings.

Inferential

3   Fill in the blanks in the sentences, using information from the text.

a   Leonardo imagined modern inventions _____ hundred years before anyone built them.

b   Leonardo's paintings were lifelike because he liked to _____ people.

c   We would not agree with Leonardo that his paintings were not _____ .

Response

4   Leonardo is often called a 'genius'. Why do you think people say this about him?

_____

5   Do you think Leonardo thought he had 'failed God and man'? Give a reason.

_____

Language Links

6   Match the phrases from the text with their meanings.

a   'a very lively and curious mind'   just like real people

b   'as a result'   a good imagination

c   'striving after perfection'   because of this

d   'very lifelike'   trying to be excellent in all he did

7   Unscramble the antonyms and pair them with words from the text.

| lively   filled   real   unusual   natural   start |

a   ldul: _____   **d**   peymt: _____

b   kefa: _____   **e**   nocmom: _____

c   nfhisi: _____   **f**   leanur: _____

Extension

Design your own invention. Label all the parts and write a brief **explanation** of how it will work. Create a class display of inventions.

Happy Holidays!

RECOUNT

Angela and her family are on a week's holiday. Angela is keeping a diary each day.
Here are some entries.

Monday: We finally arrived in Sandy Beach after the worst trip! Sophie was carsick and the car had a flat tire. Eugene didn't read the map properly and we got lost three times!

Tuesday: The girl in the cabin next to us is really nice. We went to the beach together. Mum is in bed. She says it's something she ate. We're having fish and chips for lunch and dinner. Yum!

Wednesday: Eugene managed to get a fish-hook in his finger and Dad had to take him to the hospital. Mum's still in bed. She's reading soppy stories about love. Tara (the girl next door) and I made huge ice cream sundaes for lunch.

Thursday: Sophie has a cold. She's in bed with Mum. Eugene and I are feeling fine. Eugene keeps moaning about his finger. I'm going on a picnic with Tara's family.

Friday: There was a big storm last night and the beach is covered in seaweed. The waves are still really huge and Dad can't take the boat out, so he's grumpy. Tara's family have invited Eugene and me to go to the water slides in Broad Harbour.

Literal

1   Tick 'T' if the statement is true, or 'F' if it is false.

		T	F
a	The family got lost because Dad misread the map.	○	○
b	The family is staying in Sandy Harbour.	○	○
c	Angela's mother has a cold.	○	○
d	Eugene had the fish-hook taken out in hospital.	○	○
e	Angela's new friend is Teri.	○	○
f	Angela went on a picnic to Boat Harbour.	○	○
g	The water slides are in another town.	○	○
h	Angela is feeling fine.	○	○
i	The storm was on Friday night.	○	○
j	The family has a boat.	○	○

Inferential

2 Write the answers.

a Do you think Angela is enjoying her holiday? Give some reasons.

- _____
- _____
- _____

b Are the members of Angela's family enjoying their holiday? Give some reasons.

- _____
- _____
- _____

Language Links

3 Underline the compound words in the text.

4 Form compound words by matching each word below with one from the word bank.

| sea   drift   day   sun   coast   sand   ham   life |

a _____burger

b _____break

c _____wood

d _____screen

e _____line

f _____castle

g _____shore

h _____saver

Extension

Imagine you are Angela, Eugene or Sophie. Write a **postcard** to a friend about your holiday. Don't forget to sign the postcard.

Teeth

REPORT

Have you heard of deciduous trees? They lose all their leaves in autumn and grow new ones in spring. But, have you heard of 'deciduous' teeth? Your first set of teeth can be given this name because they fall out, and new ones grow. Another name for these first teeth is 'milk teeth', and you have twenty of them. They usually begin to fall out when a child is five or six years old. New teeth replace the milk teeth until, by the time a person is twenty, they have thirty-two permanent teeth.

When you are eating your peanut butter sandwiches, your teeth have different jobs to do. The incisors and canine teeth, which are at the front of the mouth, tear the food into pieces. The premolars and molars (teeth on the sides and back of the mouth) grind up the food.

It is essential to care well for your second teeth so that they will last for a lifetime! Brushing frequently and flossing will keep them clean, and the fluoride already in the drinking water guards against getting cavities. To keep your teeth and gums healthy, you need to eat a balanced diet with adequate serves of dairy products. Dairy products, such as milk and cheese, supply calcium, which helps bones and teeth grow strong.

Literal

1   Tick 'T' if the statement is true, or 'F' if it is false.

		T	F
a	Your second teeth are called 'milk teeth'.	○	○
b	Your baby teeth all fall out.	○	○
c	You have thirty-four second teeth.	○	○
d	Canine teeth tear food into pieces.	○	○
e	Incisors grind up food.	○	○
f	Premolars and molars are on the sides and back of your mouth.	○	○
g	Calcium is added to the drinking water.	○	○
h	You usually have all your permanent teeth by age twenty.	○	○
i	Flouride helps prevent holes in your teeth.	○	○
j	Canine teeth and molars are in the front of your mouth.	○	○

Inferential

2   Match up beginnings and ends to make sentences.

a	Eating dairy products	brush after every meal.
b	If possible	helps to keep teeth really clean.
c	Flossing	aren't good for your teeth.
d	Sweets	helps teeth grow strong.

3   Are these things good or bad for your teeth? Sort them into two groups.

> cheese   chocolate   bread   meat   apples   sweets
> soft drinks   chips   milk   yoghurt   ice-blocks

GOOD   BAD

_____   _____

_____   _____

_____   _____

_____   _____

4   Answer the questions.

a   Which names for your first set of teeth are used in the text?

  i _____   ii _____   iii _____

b   Which names are used for your second set?

  i _____   ii _____

Language Links

5   Can you unscramble these sentences?

a   teeth all out your fall 'baby' _____

b   are for crunchy good apples teeth your _____

c   causes your decay holes in teeth _____

d   your strong milk teeth grow helps _____

e   good sticky are sweets not teeth your for _____

Extension

Make a **list** of uses for the millions of teeth that the Tooth Fairy collects.

NEWS REPORT

WIZARD WEEKLY

Wednesday 31 October   Established 1856

BORIS BING SIGHTED

Wanted elf criminal, Boris Bing, has been sighted in Venice. He was working as a boatman when two dwarfs on holiday spotted him.

"As soon as I saw that sly face, I knew it was Boris!" stated Dylan Dann, one of the dwarfs. When Boris realised that he had been recognised, he made his escape. Jumping overboard, he swam to land and disappeared in a crowd of tourists. He has not been seen since.

PRISONER No. 123 098

SPRITES ARE TOPS!

In recent exams, Sprites School came out on top. Students were examined on herbal lore, basic spells, broomstick skills and non-deadly potions. Sprites students scored at least A– in every subject. The school beat long-time champions, Alert Academy and Crafty College.

IRON GNOME CHALLENGE

WHEN: 29 February
WHERE: Trolltown
WHAT: 10 km swim (underwater)
80 km unicycle ride
50 km run (through tunnels)

WILLOW WANDS

Simply the best!
NOW available in –
★ beginner ★sports ★master models

Literal

1   Tick 'T' if the statement is true, or 'F' if it is false.

		T	F
a	Dylan Dan was spotted by Boris Bing.	○	○
b	Dylan is a dwarf.	○	○
c	Boris was a tourist in Venice.	○	○
d	Boris has not been captured.	○	○
e	No Sprites students scored B.	○	○
f	Alert Academy and Crafty College tied in the exams.	○	○
g	The Iron Gnome challenge is on April Fools' Day.	○	○
h	There is a 50 km unicycle ride.	○	○
i	The swim is underwater.	○	○
j	Willow wands are available in two models.	○	○

Literal

2   Write the answers.

- **a**   How did Boris get away? _____

- **b**   What subjects did Sprites students study?

    _____

- **c**   Why did they come out 'on top'?

    _____

- **d**   How do we know that Alert Academy or Crafty College usually do best
    in the exams?

    _____

Language Links

3   Look up the meanings of these words in the dictionary

- **a**   lore: _____

- **b**   potion: _____

4   Arrange these words in alphabetical order.

- **a**   witch, spell, chant, toadstool, wizard, magic, potion

    _____

- **b**   elf, gnome, troll, dwarf, ogre, pixie, sprite

    _____

- **c**   newspaper, magazine, writer, journalist, photo, advertisement, cartoon

    _____

Extension

Write another **news item** which could be included in the *Wizard Weekly*.
Your class may like to put all the items together as a class newspaper.

Working Children

REPORT

In the 18th century, very young children often had full-time jobs. In fact, some children as young as four or five worked fourteen-hour days. Many of these were orphans who had to earn their living the best way they could.

The factories in which the children worked were badly lit, stuffy and dusty. They were boiling hot in summer because there was no ventilation. In winter they were freezing cold as wind, rain and even snow blew in through cracks and broken windows.

No attempt was made to keep things safe for the workers, and accidents were common. Many children did not go home at the end of their shift but slept on the floor among the machines. When awakened early in the morning by the whistle, they quickly ate their watery porridge and commenced work again. There was no time to wash their faces or brush their hair. There was definitely no time for playing with friends! During the day, if a child became sleepy he'd be given a sharp whack on the back to wake him up again.

It is not surprising that in these conditions many children became sick and died. Others, crippled by accidents, lived out the rest of their lives as beggars. Some escaped and began lives of crime, becoming pickpockets or joining a gang of highwaymen.

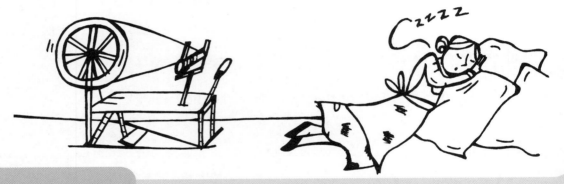

Literal

1 Circle the correct word in each set of brackets.

a   Very small children worked (part-time / full-time).

b   A child might work from six am till eight (am / pm).

c   Children sometimes slept (on the floor / in dormitories).

d   The 18th century is the (1700s / 1800s).

e   Breakfast was (thin / thick) porridge.

f   The children had (some / no) free time.

g   Children were disciplined by being (fined / hit).

h   Conditions in the factories were (terrible / fair).

i   Some children left to become (criminals / craftsmen).

Inferential

2   Write the answers.

a   Can you think why very young orphans might have been forced to work in factories?

_____

b   Why were accidents common?

_____

c   Explain in your own words why children often fell ill.

_____

d   Find evidence in the text that children were not allowed to rest.

_____

Response

3   How is your life different to that of a factory child?

_____

_____

Language Links

4   Look up the meanings of these words in the dictionary.

a   pickpocket: _____

b   highwayman: _____

c   ventilation: _____

5   Put some good descriptive words (adjectives) with these nouns. Look back at the story for ideas.

a   _____ factories   **c**   _____ machines

b   _____ days   **d**   _____ floor

Extension

Imagine that you are working in a factory in the 18th century. What is your life like? Write a **description**. You can use words in the word bank to help you.

tired	exhausted	cold	starved	ragged clothes	afraid	unhappy
whirring machines		beating	cruel boss	friends	hopeless	escape

Nat's Story (3)

HISTORICAL RECOUNT

"Hello! I thought it was you, Sir. Fancy running into you here! It's been such a long time since I saw you. Nearly ten years, isn't it?

"You're visiting friends in the area? Well, I live here now. Yes, I served my term and then I headed west. I have a little farm now and I run a few sheep. We have a cow for milk and a few chickens, and we grow vegetables and some corn for the chickens.

"Who's 'we'? Well, I'm married now. Sarah was a maid in Mr Price's house and we decided to try our luck in this new country together. Nothing for us back in old England, even if we wanted to go back.

"Yes, it's a hard life. When the seasons are bad, I do a spot of droving. Sarah has to cope on her own with the farm and the little ones. We have a little boy and a baby girl. Jack and Abigail.

"You must come to visit us. We're on the Barcoo Road. Just ask anyone for Nat and Sarah's house. It's a bark hut, not very big but I'm going to add on to it when I get the time. We've fixed it up nicely. I painted the walls white with pipe-clay before the baby was born. Sarah dyed some flour sacks and made them into curtains.

"You'll come to visit then? Good! We've just killed a sheep so we'll have a roast. I'll get Sarah to cook one of her special baked sago puddings. Goodbye, now. We'll see you tomorrow."

Literal

1   Tick 'T' if the statement is true, or 'F' if it is false.

		T	F
a	Nat has a few cows and a sheep.	○	○
b	Nat is a farmer and a drover.	○	○
c	Nat and Sarah have two boys.	○	○
d	Nat has a large farm.	○	○
e	Their house is built of clay bricks.	○	○
f	Sarah runs the farm when Jack is away.	○	○
g	Sarah worked in Mr Price's shop.	○	○
h	They grow corn to eat.	○	○

2   Write the answers.

a   Why did Nat and Sarah decide to stay in Australia? _____

_____

b How did Jack and Sarah make their home nice? _____

_____

c Why would it be difficult for Sarah when Nat went droving? _____

_____

Inferential

3 Why would Jack and Sarah's lives be hard?

_____

_____

Language Links

4 Here are some of the foods that Nat and Sarah would have eaten. Put them in alphabetical order.

> mutton   sago   barley   soda bread   damper   porridge   lamb   fish
> potatoes   golden syrup   eggs   rice   pumpkin   tapioca   bread

_____

_____

_____

Response

5 Which of these foods have you eaten?

_____

6 What are your favourite foods and why?

_____

Extension

Imagine that you are one of these:

i   an early settler like Nat or Sarah   ii   a bushranger   iii   a Cobb and Co. driver.

Write a **narrative** about an adventure you have.

Space Stories

SKILLS – IRRELEVANT INFORMATION

This text has a sentence that does not belong. It contains irrelevant or unnecessary information. Read the text and when you find the sentence, underline it.

The moon is a satellite of the Earth. This means that it orbits the Earth. The moon is about one-third the size of our planet and is 384 400 kilometres away. The Moon rotates fully in exactly the same time it takes for it to move around the Earth. This means that we always see the same face of the Moon. We never see the dark side of the Moon.

People were first able to look closely at the Moon in the 17th century. Witches are supposed to work spells at the time of the full moon. In 1609, Galileo peered through his telescope. He saw that the dark areas on the face of the "Man in the Moon" were craters. For a long time, people thought these were seas holding water and called them names such as the Sea of Tranquillity. Now we know that they are bare and empty, and were caused by meteors hitting the moon.

Literal

1   Tick 'T' if the statement is true, or 'F' if it is false.

		T	F
a	The Moon is almost 400 000 km away.	○	○
b	The Moon orbits the Sun.	○	○
c	The Moon is smaller than the Earth.	○	○
d	The craters on the Moon contain water.	○	○
e	Galileo said that meteors caused the craters.	○	○

2   Write each answer in a full sentence.

a   What is meant by saying the Moon is a satellite of Earth?

_____

b   Who first looked at the Moon through a telescope?

_____

c   Why can't we ever see the other side of the Moon?

_____

_____

*Search this text for the sentence that does not belong because it contains **irrelevant** information.*

Do you know that a shooting star may be a tiny speck of space debris, somewhere in size between a grain of sand and a little rock? How can this be? It is because of the extremely high speed at which these meteoroids travel. (Meteoroids are the pieces of debris, while meteors are the flashes of light caused by their burning up as they enter Earth's atmosphere.) Meteor showers look very pretty. Meteoroids flash to Earth at speeds between 10 and 70 km per second. They can move so rapidly because space is a vacuum and there is nothing to slow them down. But once they enter Earth's atmosphere, the matter within it causes friction on the 'shooting star'. It becomes hotter and hotter, until usually it burns up before reaching Earth.

Inferential

3   Match beginnings and ends to make true statements.

a   Meteoroids and meteors   burn up before hitting Earth.

b   We only see 'shooting stars'   are not the same thing.

c   Most meteoroids   are flashes of light.

d   Meteors   when they enter Earth's atmosphere.

Response

4   Have you seen either a 'shooting star' or an eclipse of the Moon?
     Write about what you saw.

_____

_____

_____

Extension

a   Look up the meanings of these 'space' words and phrases.

     pulsar: _____

     black hole: _____

     space junk: _____

     moon buggy: _____

b   Write a **report** on one of them.

Food from the Bush

REPORT

The early explorers of our land sometimes ran out of food on their journeys and almost starved to death. They didn't realise that even though the countryside about them looked bare, there was plenty of food if they just knew where to find it.

Even in desert areas, Indigenous Australians could always find enough food to live on. They dug in the banks of streams to find yams and they searched the bush for trees bearing fruit or berries. On the plains, they gathered grass seeds or edible roots.

If there were few big animals such as kangaroos, emus or wallabies in the area, the Indigenous Australians hunted little ones instead. They caught lizards, snakes, rats, bandicoots and small birds. Birds' eggs were another item on the menu.

The Indigenous Australians needed to gather food nearly every day because they did not have refrigerators to store it in. They took just what they needed. This was good for the trees, plants and animals too. There was no danger that the Indigenous Australians would take too much and the species become extinct.

Literal

1 Write the answers.

    a Name three large animals hunted by Indigenous Australians.

        i _____ ii _____ iii _____

    b Name three small animals hunted by Indigenous Australians.

        i _____ ii _____ iii _____

    c Name three vegetable foods gathered by Indigenous Australians.

        i _____ ii _____ iii _____

2 Complete the sentences with suitable words.

    a The early explorers did not _____ where to _____ for food in barren places.

    b Indigenous Australians could always find _____ , even in _____ .

    c Yams were found in the _____ of _____ .

    d Grass seeds were gathered on _____ and they might also find edible _____ there too.

    e _____ eggs were another source of _____ .

Inferential

3 How was the food gathering of Indigenous Australians good for the environment?

_____

_____

4 Here is a list of bush foods. Sort them into their proper groups.

possums   brush-turkey eggs   catfish   wild figs   ants   snakes   stingrays   yams
water-lily roots   wild peaches   echidnas   witchetty grubs   goose eggs   nuts   emus
nardoo seeds   Bunya pine nuts   Murray cod   lizards   grass seeds   pandanus

MEAT	FISH	EGGS	VEGETABLES/FRUIT/NUTS

Response

5 If you had been an early explorer, how would you have made sure you didn't starve?

_____

_____

Language Links

6 Find words in the text which have these meanings.

a   people seeking new lands: _____

b   a barren and dry place: _____

c   a group of animals or plants: _____

d   used to keep things cold: _____

e   disappeared completely: _____

f   able to be eaten: _____

Extension

Write a **narrative** using one of these beginnings:

• Nothing about me looked familiar. I was lost in the bush!

• Something gave the side of the tent a tremendous whack!

• "Why did I ever come camping?" I complained.

How to Keep Tadpoles

PROCEDURE

Tadpoles are great fun to keep as pets. You can easily find them in ponds and creeks, and it's absorbing to watch them grow and turn into frogs. But it's necessary to do some preparation before you go looking for them.

The first thing to do is to prepare your water. Tap water has chemicals in it, which will harm your tadpoles if you put them straight into it. So fill a large container with water and let it stand for a day.

Collect your tadpoles in a bowl or a small bucket. Don't tip out too much of the pond water. When you get home, transfer the tadpoles into an aquarium, goldfish bowl or even a large ice cream container. Tip some of the pond water in with them, and top it up with the tap water which you have had standing.

Add rocks and driftwood to the container, to make the tadpoles feel at home. You could also add some water plants from the pet shop, if you wish.

Feed your tadpoles fish food. Be careful not to give them too much because excess food will rot and make the water cloudy. Leave some of the driftwood poking out of the water, so that when the tadpoles begin to turn into frogs they have somewhere to sit. Tadpoles have gills, like fish, so they can live completely in the water. Frogs have lungs and must breathe air, so if they can't get out of the water, they'll drown. Let your tiny frogs go in a creek or pond when you see that they have completely changed.

Literal

1   Write the answers.

 a Where will you find your tadpoles?

_____

 b Explain how you will set up your tadpoles' home.

_____

_____

 c What will you feed your tadpoles? _____

 d How much food will you give them? _____

_____

Inferential

2   Fill in the gaps in the sentences with suitable words of your own.

    a   Tadpoles take in oxygen through their _____ but frogs have

    _____ .

    b   Do not feed tadpoles too _____ food.

    c   When they are grown, let your _____ go.

3   Explain why you must do these things:

    a   Let tap water stand.

    _____

    b   Leave a piece of driftwood poking out of the water.

    _____

    c   Not overfeed your tadpoles.

    _____

Response

4   If you plan to go looking for tadpoles, what should you do to keep yourself safe?

_____

_____

Language Links

5   Work out how many water creatures are listed here and then put them into alphabetical order.

        frogturtlecranetadpolewater-hendragonflyduckwater-ratheron

_____

_____

_____

Extension

Write a **procedure** for taking care of another type of pet. Remember to describe the type of preparations you may need to do before you get the pet, as well as the home, food and training it will require.

More About Max

SKILLS – PROOFREADING

There are ten mistakes in this story. Write your corrections in the box.

"Max!" called Mum. "Cindy's doll is broke. Do you know anythink about it?"

"I don't know nothing, " said Max.

"Are you shore you didn't brake it?" asked Mum.

"Well, I just lookd at it," grumbled Max. "You shouldn't of touched it," Mum replyed.

"No, I suppose your right," agreed Max. "I'm realy sorry, Mum."

CORRECTIONS

_____

_____

_____

_____

_____

_____

_____

_____

_____

Literal

1 Write the answers.

a Did Max break the doll? Give a reason for your answer.

_____

_____

b Do you think he has learned anything from his mistake? Give a reason.

_____

_____

Language Links

2 Use a word from the word bank to fill the blanks in the sentences.

| sure | shore | your | you're | break | brake |

a Max didn't intend to _____ Cindy's doll.

b The shark was seen quite close to the _____ .

c Don't touch things that are not _____ own.

d The _____ on Max's bicycle was not working.

e Max was _____ he would get into trouble.

f I know that _____ responsible for this.

There are ten mistakes in this passage. Write your corrections in the box.

"I know wear Mum has hidden the Christmas presents," said Max to his freind, Andrew. "Their under her bed. Let's look."

Thay crept into Mum's bedroom and where shaking and prodding the parsels, trying to guess what was in them. Suddenly, the door opened.

"Wot do you think your doing?" snapped Mum.

"just looking for the cat, Mum," mumbled Max as they run out the door.

CORRECTIONS

_____

_____

_____

_____

_____

_____

_____

Response

3 Write the answers.

a Why was Max silly to be looking at the presents?

_____

b Do you think Mum believed Max's excuse?

_____

Language Links

4 Match the synonyms.

a	presents	muttered
b	hidden	sneaked
c	crept	pal
d	parcel	gifts
e	mumbled	secret
f	friend	package

Extension

a What is the best Christmas present you have ever received? Write a **description** of it. Share your descriptions as a class.

b Brainstorm some ideas for Christmas presents your class could make for a local charity (nursing home, homeless shelter, hospital).

Student Profile

An important part of any teaching program is evaluation. Students need the following skills and strategies to learn to read with understanding and to develop fluency. This profile reflects the student's progress and achievements.

Skills		Assessment	
Understanding text:		Term 1 and 2	Term 3 and 4
Makes use of:	word clues		
	sentence clues		
	contextual information		
	inferential clues		
	imagining		
	enquiring		
	problem solving		
	predicting		
	researching		
	decision making based on text		
Language:	combines clauses		
	completes sentences		
	writes full sentences		
	uses language models		
Questioning:	answers questions orally		
	writes an answer		
	supplies a question for a given answer		
Puzzles:	completes word searches		
	completes cloze activities		
	unjumbles words		
	unjumbles sentences		
Instructions:	follows directions		
Dictionary skills:	knows alphabetical order		
	searches for word meanings		
	recognises nouns		
	recognises verbs		
	recognises adjectives		
	recognises adverbs		
Procedure:	orders items		
	sequences events		
Writing:	follows writing conventions and procedures		
	understands feature of genres		
	uses imagination		
	writes for specific purposes		
Prediction:	uses textual information to predict outcomes		
Reading:	reads to obtain information		
	reads for entertainment		
	deciphers non-textual materials		
	distinguishes fact from fiction		
	reads with increasing fluency		
	proofreads text, identifying errors		
	identifies main ideas		

Answers

UNIT 1   MELANIE AND LEO

a	F	b	F	c	F	d	T
e	T	f	F	g	T	h	F
i	T						

2
a   The words which tell us that Melanie has a good sense of humour are 'likes jokes'.

b   We know that Melanie is good to her friends because we are told she is kind. We know that Leo is good to his friends because we are told that he is 'loyal to friends'.

c   'Easily bored' means that Melanie doesn't like to do the same activity for long.

3

MELANIE	LEO	NEITHER
talkative	trustworthy	cranky
jolly	gentle	cruel
generous	firm	mean
funny	shy	teasing
firm	cheerful	angry

4
a   slim – skinny
b   kind – caring
c   active – busy
d   serious – thoughtful
e   bubbly – lively
f   easily – quickly
g   determined – strong-willed
h   loyal – true

UNIT 2   THE FISH KING

1
a   he felt a big tug on his line
b   he wanted to get his three wishes
c   ruby red and emerald green

2
a   The Fish King was wearing a crown of jade and pearls.
b   The Fish King said that Tom had come to visit him.
c   No, something or someone pulled him into the water.

3
a   Answers might focus on the richness of the Fish King's palace (pearls, gold, etc) or on the fact that it is under the sea (seaweed, shells, etc)
b   Teacher/Parent (answers will vary)

4
a   struggled   b   plunged
c   gasped   d   thanked
e   wondered

UNIT 3   BROOKE'S DAY

1
a   10 ½ hours   b   in the morning
c   20 minutes
d   feeding the pets and walking the dog

a	F	b	F	c	T
d	T	e	F		

3
a   yes   b   yes   c   yes
d   no   e   yes

4   Some possible answers could be: My day is like Brooke's day because I have pets I care for. My day is like Brooke's day because I do music practice too, but I play the piano not the drums. My day is not like Brooke's day because I don't have pets or do music practice, and I walk to school.

UNIT 4   MOTHS AND BUTTERFLIES

a	T	b	F	c	T	d	F
e	T	f	F	g	T	h	T
i	F	j	T	k	T		

2
a   Butterflies stomp up and down on leaves to test and taste them to see if this would be a good place to lay their eggs.
b   Laying eggs in scattered bunches protects them from enemies that might want to eat them.
c   The flowers from which Darwin's hawkmoth gets nectar are very deep, so the proboscis needs to be long to reach down into them.
d   Butterflies and moths will lose their homes if forests are cut down and may become extinct.

3
a   tidily: neatly
b   spine: backbone
c   disappeared: extinct
d   spread-out: scattered
e   stamp: stomp
f   side-by-side: together

4
a   butterflies flutter   b   mice scamper
c   ducks waddle   d   camels plod
e   bears lumber   f   rhinos charge
g   eagles soar   h   tigers prowl

UNIT 5   NAT'S STORY (1)

1
a   300 passengers
b   six months
c   a convict
d   has travelled from England

2 a	F	b	F	c	T	d	F
e	T	f	F	g	T	h	T

3   Points which could be mentioned include:
There wasn't much room.
The food was very plain and boring.
They couldn't wash or change their clothes.
The ship rolled badly in storms.
The convicts became seasick.

4   We can tell that Nat is not talking to himself because he is answering questions as he speaks.

5   The children might like to ask about Nat's family in England. They could ask if he is frightened about what will happen now.

Answers

6 a   unwell: poorly

     b   living areas: quarters

     c   frightfully: fearfully

     d   heavy weight which stops a ship from drifting: anchor

     e   people: souls

     f   closed up: cooped

     g   boiled oats: porridge

7   A 'kestrel' is a small falcon, a bird of prey.

UNIT 6   HOUDINI

1 a   Houdini was Hungarian by birth.

     b   Houdini drowned in 1926.

2 a   Houdini was thrown into the Yarra River.

     b   When Houdini was in the Yarra River, he knocked loose a body which had been trapped and it bobbed up to the surface.

     c   Houdini hoped to be the first person to fly a plane in Australia but someone flew the day before him and claimed the record.

     d   Houdini died from a burst appendix caused by someone punching him.

3   A possible reason is that he felt escaping from impossible situations required more skill than a magician's tricks did.

4 a   appear: show   b   erupt: burst

     c   impressed: excited   d   reputation: name

     e   stunt: trick   f   ambition: desire

     g   demonstrate: prove   h   obliged: agreed

UNIT 7   OUR PETS

1 a   i   6   ii   11   iii   1   iv   9

       v   1   vi   4   vii   8   viii   6

       ix   4

     b   The most popular pet is the dog.

     c   The most uncommon pets are rats and axolotls.

     d   Rabbits are as popular as fish.

     e   There are as many pet mice as there are pet guinea pigs.

     f   There are fifty pets.

2 a   Fish, birds, mice, rats and axolotls are all acceptable answers.

     b   guinea pigs, rabbits, fish, axolotls

UNIT 8   FAMILY TREE

1 a   ten   b   Mary

     c   three   d   three

     e   Harry Ross   f   six

     g   John and James   h   two

     i   Joseph O'Shea

2 a   T   b   F   c   F   d   F

     e   T   f   T   g   T

UNIT 9   WHERE DID HOT CHOCOLATE COME FROM?

1 a   F   b   T   c   T   d   F

     e   T   f   F   g   T

2 a   sugar   b   beer   c   at home

3 a   A cup of hot chocolate in the 16th century was often thick from the flour added to soak up the oil. As well, it might have had flavourings such as flower essences, wine or eggs added to it. It would be made with water instead of milk.

     b   Chocolate was imported from South America and shipping cost a lot of money, so chocolate was expensive.

     c   At a chocolate house men could talk to their friends, read the newspapers or play cards while enjoying cups of hot chocolate.

4   Possible ideas: sundae, mud cake, pudding, iced chocolate, chocolate frogs.

5 a   bitter   b   popular

     c   flavouring   d   absorb

     e   stodgy   f   expensive

6   [2] Add... [4] Pour... [3] Add... [5] Finally... [1] Put...

UNIT 10   MY NANNA

1 a   She made a parachute jump.

     b   Nan was sixty-eight.

     c   Nan has had to give up running marathons.

     d   She doesn't have time for running.

     e   Nan would like to learn to fly a plane.

     f   Nan's skiing is sublime.

     g   Nan swims, surfs and sails.

     h   She always has time for her grandchild.

2 a   Nan wears leather when she rides her bike for protection.

     b   The person speaking in the poem is Nan's grandchild.

     c   Nan does all of these things because she has a lot of energy.

     d   Mum and Dad are worried by Nan's activities.

3   Suitable adjectives are: enthusiastic, energetic, busy, cheerful

4 a   roars: travels   b   sublime: skilful

     c   amazing: surprising

     d   disapproving: unhappy

     e   busy: active   f   spend: use

UNIT 11   APRIL FOOLS' DAY

1 a   Susan   b   Jo

     c   Jason told Susan there was a parcel for her.

     d   Tom told Brooke she was wearing pyjamas.

2 a   F   b   T   c   F

     d   T   e   T

3 a Tom approved of the trick Jason played on Susan. He thought it was 'cunning'.

   b Susan was annoyed by the trick Jason played on her.

   c We know because she was in a bad mood and didn't talk to Tom.

   d Tom's trick didn't work because Brooke had already been fooled by Jo, and so she was on her guard.

4 A suggested answer for this is: The best trick was the one Jo played on Brooke because the way that Brooke rushed to see the unicorn sounds funny.

5 a fooled   b foolish

   c foolery   d foolishly

UNIT 12 JUMARI

1 a Jumari is ten years of age. [F]

   b Three people live in Jumari's house. [F]

   c Jumari lives on the island of Lombok. [T]

   d Supomo is learning to be a farmer. [F]

   e Jumari is now in school. [T]

   f Supomo is Jumari's big brother. [T]

   g Supomo lives beside the sea. [T]

   h Jumari's house has electricity. [F]

2 a Jumari hopes to stay in school all this year.

   b Jumari has sometimes had to drop out to help her mother.

   c Jumari was helped in her schoolwork by her friends.

   d Jumari did not fall behind in her work.

   e The family fetched their water from the well.

   f The house is made of bamboo.

   g The family grows rice.

3 a Jumari's house is of bamboo and it is not in good condition. In some parts the walls and roof are broken.

   b Jumari and her mother do not have enough money to fix it up.

   c Possible reasons for 'yes' are: i Jumari seems to have a hard life because she has to work hard with chores or helping in the fields. ii Her house is falling apart and does not have gas, electricity or running water. iii She cannot count on being able to go to school all the time.

4 Suitable adjectives are: determined, hardworking and poor.

5 Some possible ways are:

- Jumari's house doesn't have gas, electricity or running water.
- Jumari has to walk to a well to get water.
- Jumari sometimes has to drop out of school to help in the fields.
- Jumari is very poor.
- Jumari's house is made from bamboo.

6 a slim   b seaside   c rotting

   d connected   e ache   f progress

UNIT 13 GRANDMA'S SCHOOLDAYS

1 a F   b F   c T   d T

   e F   f F   g T

2 a Olga's father might have worked on the railway.

   b Half-time schools were set up in places where there weren't enough children to have a full-time school open all the time.

   c You would only have to go to school two days one week and three weeks the next.

   d You might not learn as much as a student in a full-time school.

3 Some differences are:

- Not all schools opened all the time.
- The teacher might ride a horse to school.
- There were no school canteens.
- Children might walk many kilometres to school.
- Children sometimes didn't wear shoes to school.

4 a milliner: someone who makes hats.

   b stubble: short bits of grain left after harvesting.

   c mutton: meat from sheep.

5 The five compound words are: railway, juice-packs, homemade, half-time, full-time

UNIT 14 HOW TO MAKE A VOLCANO

1 a F   b T   c F   d T

   e F   f T   g F   h T

   i F   j T

2 a Red colour is used because lava is red.

   b This could be messy when the lava flows so it would be best to do this outside.

3 a after   b Before

   c before   d before

4 a cram   b place   c tightly

   d push   e dye   f drips

   g thoughtfully   h rapidly   i explode

   j container

UNIT 15 WHERE WILL WE GO?

1 a Cameron was Bradon's friend.

   b The old car had 'blown up' (Something very serious had gone wrong with the old car.)

   c Nan has had a knee operation.

   d The tent has not been used for a long time so it might have some holes.

2 a Disneyland:

   FOR

   Cameron's family enjoyed it.

   AGAINST

   It would be too expensive, as the family has already bought a new car.

b   Nan and Pop's:
     FOR
     The children love it.
     AGAINST
     Nan has had a knee operation and might
     not be able to look after visitors.
c   The beach:
     FOR
     It would be cheap.
     AGAINST
     The tent might have holes.

3   a   yes   b   yes   c   yes
     d   no   e   no

4   A possible answer could be: I think the family
     should go to the beach and camp in the tent
     because they will make lots of new friends in the
     camping ground.

5   a   pay for   b   gloomy   c   delay
     d   kept

UNIT 16   ABOUT MAX

The corrections are:
voice, been, haven't, mice, would have been,
chocolate, don't, noticing, story, there

1   a   It was Cindy's birthday.
     b   Max said that mice might have nibbled at the
          cake.
     c   Mum knew that Max had eaten some icing
          because he had it all around his mouth.

2   SINGULAR   PLURAL
     mouse   mice
     deer   deer
     foot   feet
     tooth   teeth
     cherry   cherries
     fox   foxes
     goose   geese
     church   churches
     baby   babies
     woman   women
     roof   roofs
     volcano   volcanoes

3   Cindy felt upset.
4   Mum probably felt sympathetic.
5   Mum probably felt angry.
6   We know that Max is sorry for what he has done
     because he looks down and thinks, 'Oh dear' to
     himself.
7   a   To be brave: to keep your chin up
     b   To panic: to lose your head
     c   To listen well: to be all ears
     d   To agree: to see eye to eye
     e   To watch: to keep an eye on someone
     f   To put on a strange expression: to make
          a face

UNIT 17   OUR EARS

1   a   T   b   F   c   F   d   T
     e   T   f   F   g   F

2   a   The middle ear picks up vibrations from
          sound and passes them on to the inner ear.
     b   The inner ear has tubes filled with fluid that
          move when we move. Nerves tell the brain
          about the movement and the brain tells the
          muscles we need to keep our balance.

3   a   120 decibels   b   30 decibels
     c   60 decibels   d   40 decibels

4   a   harm: danger   b   moves: transfers
     c   quivers: vibrates   d   cylinders: tubes
     e   always: constantly   f   keep safe: protect

5   a   earmuffs: warm ear coverings
     b   earache: a pain in the ear
     c   earring: an ornament for the ear
     d   earbash: to talk without pausing
     e   earwig: an insect

UNIT 18   STRANGE ENDINGS

1   a   William's apothecary embalmed his body.
     b   The modern name for apothecary is chemist.
     c   Nelson was a famous English admiral.
     d   Jeremy Bentham was a thinker.
     e   His body was taken out of its display case and
          sat on a chair during meetings.

2   a   Nelson's   b   William's
     c   Bentham's   d   William's

3   a   solve   b   stomachs   c   clever
     d   bizarre   e   fright

4   Possible answers might be: I would have felt sick
     at the terrible smell and would have rushed out of
     the church to get away from it. I would wonder
     why people were rushing out of the church. I
     wouldn't want to see what the body looked like!

5   a   conquer: to overcome or defeat
     b   embalmed: preserved from decay by use
          of chemicals or herbs
     c   decomposing: rotting, decaying
     d   barrel: a large, round wooden container
     e   dissected: cut up for examination

UNIT 19   THE BULLIES

1   a   Kevin was afraid to go to school because
          he was being bullied.
     b   Possible answers are:
          • The bullies might hide his schoolbag.
          • They might throw his books in the dirt.
          • They might steal his lunch.
          • They might throw some of his lunch away.
          • They might take his lunch money.
          • They might trip him up.
          • They might throw his cap on the road.
     c   William didn't listen because Kevin was
          stuttering too much.

d Kevin's father was watching a football match on television and didn't want to be interrupted.

e The bullies threatened Kevin that even worse things would happen to him if he told anyone.

2 a T b T c F
d T e F

3 a Kevin is very unhappy.
b Bullies make children afraid.
c Teachers can help to stop bullies.
d Bullying must be stopped.

4 knew, worried, questioned, troubles, headmaster, parents, meeting, bullying

5 Possible answers are: Kevin felt very relieved when the bullying stopped. Kevin was pleased that he had told his mother about the problem. Kevin realised that he would never have solved the problem on his own.

UNIT 20   THE HAUNTED HOUSE

1 a F b T c T d F
e F f T g F h T

2 a You will find your friend and leave the house.
b You will find a vampire in there.
c You will fall through the rotten floorboards.
d You will run out of the house.
e You will find treasure.
f You will be eaten by a lion.

3 a unlocked: unfastened b nerve: courage
c rotten: crumbling d decide: choose
e investigate: search f balcony: verandah

4 a blood-curdling / spine-chilling / heart-stopping
b spine-chilling / heart-stopping
c faint-hearted
d blood-curdling / spine-chilling / heart-stopping

UNIT 21   ANTS

a T b F c F d T
e F f T g F h T
i F j F

2 1500 kg

3 A 'predator' is an animal or insect which attacks and eats another animal or insect.

4 A good answer might be: The handmaidens have the most important job because they care for the queen. Without the queen there would not be a colony, because there would not be any eggs.

5 Good choices are: busy, strong, brave

6 a pincers: jaws b invasion: attack
c colonies: settlements d brave: fearless
e damage: harm

7 a antelope b anteater
c Antarctic d antler
e anthem f antonym

UNIT 22   NAT'S STORY (2)

1 a F b T c F d F
e T f T g T

2 a The shop sells padlocks, penknives, shawls, spices, muskets, mustard, meat choppers, corsets and many other items.
b Nat hopes to farm some land west of the Blue Mountains.
c He will do this when he finishes his term in four years' time.

3 a He learns a lot about the outside world.
b The words are 'was it crowded'.

4 Mr Price's shop was different because it sold a very wide range of goods. Shops today usually sell one type of goods.

5 Acceptable answers could be: I would like Nat's job because he sold so many different things that I would not be bored. I would not like Nat's job because he worked very long hours and I would get too tired.

6 a assign b corset c penknife
d musket e mustard f shawl

UNIT 23   CHRISTOPHER

1 a F b T c F d T
e F f T g F h F

2 a 'My personality's sparkling'
b 'My manners are refined'
c '… a brilliant mind'
d 'I never shirk a dare'
e 'I'm loyal and kind and fair'
f 'My sporting skills are swell'
g 'I'm modest too as well'

3 Never judge a book by its cover.

4 Child can choose any quality but must justify choice, e.g. I like the way Christopher never shirks a dare because he would be an interesting and exciting person to spend time with.

5 a attractive b warty
c harmful d important
e adventurous f charming
g courageous h musical

UNIT 24   BEAVERS

1 a to make the water deeper
b clumsy on land, graceful in water
c to keep the water out
d underground

2 a The sharp, front teeth are 'incisors'.
b The entrance is underwater so that enemies cannot get in easily.
c Beavers will smack the water with their tails to alert other beavers of danger. A mother beaver will protect her baby from danger by holding it between her teeth and swimming away as quickly as she can.

3	a	thickly	b	skilfully		
	c	speedily	d	strongly		
5	a	fur	b	tails	c	paws
	d	pause	e	fir	f	tales

UNIT 25 SCRAMBLED STORIES

The correct order for the story is:
We have a naughty kitten named Tosca. She thinks she is a fierce lion and if a dog comes into our garden, she rushes at it, hissing and snarling. She doesn't realise that she is a weak little kitten and that she should hide. One day, Cassie, a black Labrador, wandered into our garden. Tosca rushed at Cassie. Cassie was not frightened of a small, grey kitten and going up to Tosca, gave her a huge lick. Tosca was so amazed that she raced up the nearest tree. She didn't come down until dinnertime.

1   a   growling: snarling
     b   surprised: amazed
     c   strayed: wandered
     d   wild: fierce
     e   afraid: frightened
     f   charged: rushed

2   Teacher/Parent

3   [6] Half-way... [2] She did not... [1] Anna was given... [3] Foolishly... [11] Anna needed... [8] She banged... [7] Near... [5] But then... [10] They took... [4] She started... [9] Anna's parents...

4   a   Anna was foolish to try skating down a steep hill before she had learned to skate well and to be able to brake and stop.
     b   (Various answers.) A lesson I could learn from Anna's experience is not to try to do too much too quickly.
     c   (Various answers.) I would tell them to learn on a flat surface before trying to skate down hills.
     d   (Various answers.) Anna's parents would have felt very worried and upset when they were called. They might have been annoyed with Anna for being foolish.

5   a   rapidly: slowly   b   base: top
     c   finished: began   d   wisely: foolishly
     e   summit: bottom   f   low: high

UNIT 26 TORY'S GOOD IDEA

1   a   Tory thought that her mother watched television and that she ate whatever she liked.
     b   They swapped one day in the long holidays.
     c   Mum was planning to go to Jenny's house to swim and have lunch.

2   a   Mum   b   had no idea
     c   exhausted

3   Kitchen: wash up, wash kitchen floor. Bathroom: clean bath and bathroom basin, wash bathroom floor, change towels. Bedroom: vacuum bedrooms, make beds. Loungeroom: dust loungeroom furniture, vacuum carpet in loungeroom. Laundry: do washing, do ironing. Other: feed pets, make Dad's lunch, do shopping, empty waste-paper bins. (Make Dad's lunch and feed pets could also be categorised under kitchen.)

4   The things to be cleaned up: put curtain back on rail, tidy cupboards and close up open bags or put into containers, wash up, close fridge, clean up pet dish, pick up items from floor, wash floor, tidy drawers and close them, clean stove and cupboard tops.

UNIT 27 DO HIGH BUILDINGS SWAY IN THE WIND?

1   a   T   b   F   c   T   d   T
     e   F   f   T   g   T   h   F
     i   T

2   a   If a building moves too much, the people in it will feel uncomfortable and may even become sick.
     b   The computer knows which way the wind will push the building and the weight moves to the other side to keep the building from moving.

3   Various answers. Possible answers could be:
I would like to live in a multi-storey building because I would be able to see all over the city.
I would not like to live in a multi-storey building because I am afraid of heights.

4   a   violently   b   gusts
     c   damage   d   occupants
     e   cores   f   technique
     g   connected

5   a   escalator   b   sculptor
     c   gable   d   farm

UNIT 28 LEONARDO DA VINCI

1   Leonardo's paintings were very lifelike.

2   Leonardo's wife was called Mona Lisa.

3   a   four   b   watch   c   good

4   Leonardo imagined so many of the things which have become part of the modern world.
No one else had ideas like this.

5   Leonardo did not live up to his own high standards but people for hundreds of years have appreciated the beautiful paintings he created.
So he did not fail.

6   a   a good imagination
     b   because of this
     c   trying to be excellent in all he did
     d   just like real people

7   a   dull: lively   b   fake: natural
    c   finish: start   d   empty: filled
    e   common: unusual   f   unreal: real

UNIT 29   HAPPY HOLIDAYS!

a F   b F   c F   d T
e F   f F   g T   h T
i F   j T

2   a   Possible reasons for 'yes' are: She has made a friend. She is enjoying the food. She has been on a picnic. She is going to the water-slides. She is not sick.
    b   Possible reasons for 'no' are: Mum has been sick. Sophie has become sick. Dad hasn't been able to fish as much as he wants to. Eugene has injured his finger.

3   Compound words are: carsick, fish-hook, ice cream, seaweed, water slides.

4   a   hamburger   b   daybreak
    c   driftwood   d   sunscreen
    e   coastline   f   sandcastle
    g   seashore   h   lifesaver

UNIT 30   TEETH

a F   b T   c F   d T
e F   f T   g F   h T
i T   j F

2   a   Eating dairy products helps teeth grow strong.
    b   If possible brush after every meal.
    c   Flossing helps to keep teeth really clean.
    d   Sweets aren't good for your teeth.

3   GOOD: cheese, bread, meat, apples, milk, yoghurt.
BAD: chocolate, sweets, soft drinks, chips, ice-blocks

4   a   i   deciduous   ii   milk   iii   baby
    b   i   permanent   ii   second

5   a   Your 'baby' teeth all fall out.
    b   Crunchy apples are good for your teeth.
    c   Decay causes holes in your teeth.
    d   Milk helps your teeth grow strong.
    e   Sticky sweets are not good for your teeth.

UNIT 31   WIZARD WEEKLY

1   a F   b T   c F   d T
    e T   f F   g F   h F
    i T   j F

2   a   Boris leapt overboard and swam away.
    b   The students studied herbal lore, basic spells, broomstick skills and non-deadly potions.
    c   The students all scored at least A– in every subject.
    d   These schools are called 'long-time champions'.

4   a   chant, magic, potion, spell, toadstool, witch, wizard

    b   dwarf, elf, gnome, ogre, pixie, sprite, troll
    c   advertisement, cartoon, journalist, magazine, newspaper, photo, writer

UNIT 32   WORKING CHILDREN

1   a   full-time   b   pm
    c   on the floor   d   1700s
    e   thin   f   no
    g   hit   h   terrible
    i   criminals

2   a   There was no one to look after them so they needed to work to live.
    b   The bosses did nothing to keep the children safe from dangerous machines.
    c   The children slept on the floor. They ate badly. They did not get out in the sunshine and fresh air. They did not even wash.
    d   There was no time for play and if a child stopped working, he or she was smacked to make them begin working again.

3   Children's answers might cover such issues as not needing to work, going to school, eating properly and sleeping in a proper bed.

5   Some possible answers are:
    a   dirty, dusty, dim, crowded
    b   exhausting, long, miserable, tiring
    c   noisy, dangerous, whirring, huge
    d   dirty, cold, hard, dusty

UNIT 33   NAT'S STORY (3)

1   a F   b T   c F   d F
    e F   f T   g F   h F

2   a   They felt that they would have a better life in Australia.
    b   Nat painted the walls white with pipe-clay and Sarah dyed some flour sacks and made them into curtains.
    c   Sarah would have to look after a baby and a small child as well as looking after the animals on the farm.

3   They had to grow their own food and they did not have much money. They might have to cope with droughts and floods. Life would be hard for Sarah when Jack was away. They would have to work hard all the time.

4   barley, bread, carrots, damper, eggs, fish, golden syrup, lamb, mutton, porridge, potatoes, pumpkin, rice, sago, soda-bread, tapioca

5   Teacher/Parent

6   Teacher/Parent

UNIT 34   SPACE STORIES

The sentence which does not belong is: Witches are supposed to work spells at the time of the full moon.

1   a T   b F   c T
    d F   e F

Answers

2 a The moon makes a circular path around the Earth.

b Galileo first looked through a telescope at the moon.

c The Moon takes the same amount of time to turn on its axis as it does to orbit the Earth. This means that it always shows the same face to us.
The sentence which does not belong is: Meteor showers look very pretty.

3 a Meteoroids and meteors are not the same thing.

b We only see 'shooting stars' when they enter Earth's atmosphere.

c Most meteoroids burn up before hitting Earth.

d Meteors are flashes of light.

4 Teacher/Parent

UNIT 35 FOOD FROM THE BUSH

1 a i kangaroos ii wallabies iii emus

b i rats ii bandicoots
iii small birds

c i yams ii grass seeds
iii edible roots

2 a know, search b food, deserts

c banks, streams d plains, roots

e Birds', food

3 Indigenous Australians only took as much food as they needed, so the plants and animals were not used up completely.

4 MEAT: possums, snakes, echidnas, witchetty grubs, emus, lizards, ants
FISH: catfish, Murray cod, stingrays
EGGS: brush-turkey eggs, goose eggs
VEGETABLES, FRUIT, NUTS: wild figs, water-lily roots, wild peaches, nardoo seeds, Bunya Pine nuts, pandanus nuts, yams, grass seeds

5 Answers might suggest such things as leaving food in caches for the return journey, making friends with the Indigenous Australians or learning from Indigenous Australians before you left.

6 a explorers b desert c species

d refrigerator e extinct f edible

UNIT 36 HOW TO KEEP TADPOLES

1 a Tadpoles can be found in ponds and creeks.

b Tadpoles can be kept in a large ice-cream container, a goldfish bowl or an aquarium. Put some pond water in, together with tap water that has stood for a while. Add rocks, stones and driftwood. You could put in some water plants too.

c Tadpoles can eat fish food.

d Only give them as much as they eat quickly.

2 a gills, lungs b much c frogs

3 a This is so the water is the same temperature as the pond water.

b When the tadpoles turn into frogs they need somewhere to sit.

c Uneaten food will rot and make the water cloudy.

4 Answers could include going with an older person, being careful at the edge of streams so you don't fall in and not wading in streams or ponds because there might be rubbish on the bottom which could cut your feet.

5 crane, dragonfly, duck, frog, heron, tadpole, turtle, water-hen, water-rat

UNIT 37 MORE ABOUT MAX

The corrections are: broken, anything, I don't know anything, sure, break, looked, shouldn't have, replied, you're, really.

1 a Yes, Max did break it because he admitted it at the end.

b Yes, he has because he is sorry for what he did and probably won't do it again.

2 a break b shore c your

d brake e sure f you're

The corrections are: where, friend, They're, They, were, parcels, What, you're, Just, ran.

3 a He was spoiling the surprise he would get on Christmas Day.

b No, because they were just where the presents had been hidden.

4 a presents: gifts b hidden: secret

c crept: sneaked d parcel: package

e mumbled: muttered f friend: pal